## Praise for *Succeeding at Seminary*

Anyone called to ministry should read this book. Anyone! In it are nuggets of wisdom that will help one start, run, and finish the race well. I will be quick to recommend it to prospective seminarians.

> **DANIEL L. AKIN**, president, Southeastern Baptist Theological Seminary

This easily digestible work is both timeless and timely. Potential seminarians, you need to be asking every question listed in these pages. I found myself wishing that it had been written in 1991, when I needed it the most. Thanks to Jason Allen, you need not have any such regrets.

> **BART BARBER**, pastor, First Baptist Church Farmersville, TX

Compelling, clear, and concise, *Succeeding at Seminary* is a remarkably helpful resource for those seeking to prepare for a lifetime of faithful Christian service. Kudos to Jason Allen for recognizing that a call to ministry includes a call to preparation and for providing such careful and thoughtful guidance regarding the importance of study, theological conviction, personal and family commitments, the place of church and friendship, as well as mission and ministry. Church leaders should keep several copies of this little book on hand to give to men and women contemplating God's call on their lives. Highly and heartily recommended!

> **DAVID S. DOCKERY**, president, International Alliance for Christian Education and Distinguished Professor of Theology, Southwestern Seminary

For all prospective or present seminary students, this book is a priceless gem and a must-read. Jason K. Allen, one of our generation's most outstanding seminary presidents, has laid out a brilliant case for making the most of your theological education. Well-developed and practically applied, Allen will help you strategically maximize your seminary training. I urge you to read and follow this book's insightful wisdom and sound advice.

**STEVEN J. LAWSON**, president, OnePassion Ministries; professor, The Master's Seminary, teaching fellow, Ligonier Ministries

This book serves the health of tomorrow's church. We need men who aspire to the work of pastor-elder and get a focused season of training to acquire the skills they will need to preach and teach well for a lifetime. Seminary is not about filling your freezer with fish but learning how to fish for yourself—acquiring the mindset and abilities you need to keep reading and learning and freshly teaching God's Word for decades. I love that Jason shares this vision—and that he checks our subjective sense of "call" with the objective reality of marriage. If you are married, that calling is clearer and surer than any "call to ministry" you may be pursuing. From beginning to end, this book rings with such wisdom, and will not only help you stay Christian in seminary but perhaps even find what it means to flourish in this important season.

**DAVID MATHIS**, executive editor, desiringGod.org; pastor, Cities Church, Saint Paul; adjunct professor, Bethlehem College & Seminary, Minneapolis; author, *Habits of Grace: Enjoying Jesus through the Spiritual Disciplines*; coauthor, *How to Stay Christian in Seminary*

This is exactly the right book for seminary students—or anyone considering a call to ministry. Jason Allen wonderfully combines the most practical observations and the most passionate encouragement for those called to serve the church—and are therefore called to prepare for that service. Sound wisdom is found here, and Jason Allen writes not only as a seminary president, but as one who knows the student experience firsthand.

**R. ALBERT MOHLER JR.**, president, The Southern Baptist Theological Seminary

Many students have questions about preparing for seminary and about whether they should attend seminary. Jason Allen's book on succeeding at seminary is a must-read for students thinking about going to seminary, planning to go to seminary, and for those already in seminary. The book exudes the kind of wisdom we find in Proverbs and is full of the practical advice that is fitting for those who desire to live in a godly and mature way during their seminary years. I recommend this work with enthusiasm.

**THOMAS R. SCHREINER**, James Buchanan Harrison Professor of New Testament Interpretation, Associate Dean, The Southern Baptist Theological Seminary, Louisville, KY

Jason Allen knows how seminary works. His experience as a student, professor, pastor, and administrator gives him unique and comprehensive insights into the seminarian adventure. When God calls you to preach (or to church leadership of any kind), God calls you to prepare. If you are thinking about committing to this level of preparation, you should read this book first.

**JIMMY SCROGGINS**, Lead Pastor, Family Church, West Palm Beach, FL

For an aspiring minister, where to attend seminary is a defining decision. It should not be made lightly. Drawing from seasoned experience, Jason Allen will help you ask the right questions not only for choosing a seminary but also for getting the most out of it while you're there. *Succeeding at Seminary* brims with practical wisdom for the journey. Read it and benefit.

**MATT SMETHURST**, managing editor, The Gospel Coalition; author, *Deacons: How They Serve and Strengthen the Church* and *Before You Open Your Bible: Nine Heart Postures for Approaching God's Word*

# Succeeding at Seminary

12 KEYS
TO GETTING
THE MOST
OUT OF YOUR
THEOLOGICAL
EDUCATION

## Jason K. Allen

**MOODY PUBLISHERS**
CHICAGO

© 2021 by
JASON K. ALLEN

Some content in this book was adapted from the author's blog posts (jasonkallen .com).

Scripture quotations taken from the (NASB®) New American Standard Bible®, Copyright © 1960, 1971, 1977, 1995, 2020 by The Lockman Foundation. Used by permission. All rights reserved. www.lockman.org

Edited by Matt Smethurst
Interior design: Erik M. Peterson and Kaylee Lockenour
Cover design: Gabriel Reyes-Ordeix
Cover image of man sitting by Drew Coffman on Unsplash.

Library of Congress Cataloging-in-Publication Data

Names: Allen, Jason K., author.
Title: Succeeding at seminary : 12 keys to getting the most out of your
   theological education / Jason K. Allen.
Description: Chicago : Moody Publishers, [2021] | Includes bibliographical
   references. | Summary: "Seminary is an important step toward
   ministry-but only when you make the most of it. Prepare for your calling
   and make the most of your theological training with Succeeding at
   Seminary. Seminary president Jason K. Allen provides guidance for
   incoming and current seminary students on how to maximize their
   education experience. You'll learn how to select the right institution
   and weigh the pros and cons of online or in-person classes. You'll also
   receive tips for developing rapport with peers and professors and get
   insights for how to navigate a work, study, and family-life balance to
   help you survive the rigors of advanced theological learning"-- Provided
   by publisher.
Identifiers: LCCN 2020047538 (print) | LCCN 2020047539 (ebook) | ISBN
   9780802426321 (paperback) | ISBN 9780802499615 (ebook)
Subjects: LCSH: Theology--Study and teaching.
Classification: LCC BV4020 .A45 2021 (print) | LCC BV4020 (ebook) | DDC
   230.071/1--dc23
LC record available at https://lccn.loc.gov/2020047538
LC ebook record available at https://lccn.loc.gov/2020047539

Originally delivered by fleets of horse-drawn wagons, the affordable paperbacks from D. L. Moody's publishing house resourced the church and served everyday people. Now, after more than 125 years of publishing and ministry, Moody Publishers' mission remains the same—even if our delivery systems have changed a bit. For more information on other books (and resources) created from a biblical perspective, go to www.moodypublishers.com or write to:

Moody Publishers
820 N. LaSalle Boulevard
Chicago, IL 60610

1 3 5 7 9 10 8 6 4 2

*Printed in the United States of America*

This book is affectionately dedicated to my first pastorate, Muldraugh Baptist Church.

No congregation has ever afforded a young minister a more loving and supportive first church than you did me. You believed in me, supported me, invested in me, and believed the best about me. You received my preaching, supported my family, and followed my leadership, all the while overlooking my many shortcomings.

You supported me while I completed my Master of Divinity degree and encouraged me to pursue my PhD. Quite literally, through your faithfulness, accommodation, and generosity, you enabled us to succeed at seminary. We are—and forever will be—profoundly grateful.

And most especially to Bud and Pat Watts, Ed and Barbara Carroll, and Bill and Kelli Wilson. You took us in like family, supported us like dependents, and served us like dear friends. Daily, you demonstrated the love of Christ to us—making our first pastorate not just manageable, but delightful.

Karen and I remain grateful beyond measure for all you did for us then, and for all you continue to mean to us now. Thank you.

# Contents

# Foreword

If you have picked up this book to help think through your choice of seminary, or to think about whether to go to seminary or not, or to think through important aspects or factors in your ministry preparation, I believe that you will find Dr. Allen's counsel both wise and timely.

Your sense of calling to ministry—and especially the church's confirmation of your sincere desire to promote the glory of God in the gospel of His Son, by evangelism and discipleship—are vital to your benefiting from formal theological education. Dr. Allen helpfully provides you some tools for self-reflection and assessment in this area.

He also explains what seminary is, what it is for, and why it matters. That, too, is important for you to understand if you are to fully benefit from what this experience has to offer. And his questions for picking a place to study are very, very good.

Dr. Allen gives you a careful and fair presentation about the importance and advantages of in-person theological education, as well as the pluses and minuses of online study. He reminds you of the crucial nexus of life and doctrine in your preparation, counsels you on growing in your stewardship of time and attending to your home life, as well as being wise with your finances—all vital matters and areas for you to consider.

In fact, I don't think there is a wasted word in this book. If you are considering seminary, you really do need to pray and think through all the issues that are raised here, and pay heed to all the wise and godly counsel that Dr. Allen offers.

True confession: I like to read books about how prospective seminarians should think through their choices about, make use of the opportunities afforded by, and be aware of the challenges involved in formal theological education for ministry preparation. There are a number of reasons that I have this inclination. I'll mention two. First, I have been involved in theological education for over half my life. And I am always trying to improve what I am providing our students, so reading these kinds of good books helps me think hard about what I am doing and how I can do it better. Second, I like to read books like this because I talk to prospective theological students all the time, and I want to give them sound and thorough counsel.

I especially like to read books on this topic by those who are experienced and faithful, and my friend Dr. Jason Allen is both of those things. I trust him, and love to learn from him. And this book has already helped me. I will be using what I have learned here to help prospective students make the best possible informed decisions for their ministry preparation. It will help you too. I'm sure of it.

LIGON DUNCAN
Chancellor and CEO, Reformed Theological Seminary
John E. Richards Professor of Systematic and
Historical Theology

# Introduction

I remember my seminary journey well. Even though more than two decades have passed, it seems like yesterday when my wife, Karen, and I were weighing whether to attend seminary—and, after that, which one.

We felt as though we were standing on the edge of an embankment and before us was the vast unknown. We were certain God had called me to ministry and that ministry preparation was essential, but we were uncertain of most everything else. For Karen and me, a step of faith was not just appropriate, it was unavoidable.

We sensed that a call to ministry included seminary studies, but we had little idea of what that would entail. Though we enjoyed a fruitful ministry role in our hometown of Mobile, Alabama, we believed God was calling me to attend seminary. Even still, we had more questions than answers. We could see the future, but only dimly.

After seeking wise counsel, exploring several institutions, and familiarizing myself with all that seminary training would entail, we determined fall 2001 would be D-Day. We prayed, strategized, and mobilized with that move date in sight. We loaded our belongings into a twenty-six-foot U-Haul and drove north for theological training. My calling was real, and now so was the move it prompted.

Our departure day started inauspiciously. Before even pulling out of the driveway, our U-Haul exhibited engine trouble. Yet we slogged along, trudging our way north on Interstate 65 to Southern Seminary in Louisville, Kentucky. When we finally arrived, we were both wearied and exhilarated, fatigued but faith-filled for the journey before us.

We unloaded into our small, second-floor apartment and soon began undertaking new jobs, making new friends, joining a new church, and immersing ourselves in a new campus community.

**For those called to ministry, preparation is nonnegotiable; and for most, that will include seminary studies.**

Everything felt new, but the road of ministry preparation was (and is) as old as the church itself. Throughout the New Testament, a clear pattern of ministry preparation emerges. The Lord calls His servants to ministry, and they are to be equipped as they pursue that service.

Karen and I now look back on that season of life with laughter at our naivete, with joy on the healthy seminary experience God gave us, and with a sense of sobriety at all that was—and is—at stake. For those called to ministry, preparation is nonnegotiable; and for most, that will include seminary studies.

As we will see in the pages ahead, formal seminary education is not a prerequisite for gospel ministry, but sufficient ministry preparation most certainly is. And the conventional way of receiving this training is in the context of a biblically faithful seminary.

To benefit from a healthy seminary experience, you must consider at least three questions: whether to attend seminary, which seminary to attend, and how to get the most out of the experience.

Though all three considerations are important, this book is not so much an argument for why you should attend seminary, though we will touch on that. This book is more of an instruction manual for picking your course of study and optimizing your seminary experience.

Your personal investment—of money, time, and energy—is too great not to pursue the highest return possible. The ministry entrusted to you is too consequential not to be as thoroughly prepared as possible.

As we will see in this book, you can—you must!—have a healthy seminary experience. Resolve, then, to succeed at seminary. Read along with me and learn the ins and outs of theological education, explore more fully God's call on your life and the ministry before you, and discover how to get the most out of your seminary experience. Your call to ministry is too momentous to settle for anything less.

# CHAPTER 1

# Celebrate and Clarify Your Call

Congratulations! The fact that you're reading this book likely means you sense a call to ministry. A calling is a singular opportunity, a precious stewardship. You are embarking on one of the most joy-filled, consequential lives you can live.

To be clear, the call to follow Christ is universal—to be issued by believers to all people, at all times, and in all places. All people must hear the gospel call because God intends it for all people (Matt. 28:18–19).

But God's call to ministry is different—it is selective, individual, and specific. God enlists ministers into a conscripted force and equips them to serve His church, teach His Word, and proclaim His gospel. Therefore, if you have been called to ministry, God has sovereignly set you apart for His service.

I begin this book by pointing out the singularity of your call not to foster pride or fear within you. Rather, my goal is to remind you of the uniqueness of your call, to awaken you accordingly, and to prompt you to pursue it with maturity and faithfulness.

## THE BEST INVITATION

Invitations are common to human experience. We receive them from all sorts of people to all sorts of events: graduations, weddings, office parties, baby showers, dinner gatherings, and so on. We've grown accustomed to it.

Yet some invitations eclipse all others—such as, say, an invitation to the White House. In fact, etiquette expert Emily Post famously observed, "An invitation to the White House is a must attend. You must drop everything and go."[1] A number of years ago, I received a White House invitation and, believe me, I prioritized it accordingly.

As grand as such an invitation is, an invitation to ministry is grander still. God, who issues the call, is infinitely greater than the president of the United States. The location—fields white for harvest (John 4:35)—is far superior to the White House. And, of course, the work of ministry is far more noble and lasting than anything happening at 1600 Pennsylvania Avenue—regardless of who occupies the address.

## THE HIGH CALL OF MINISTRY

This is a book about preparing—especially in seminary—for the ministry God has called you to undertake. Before we get ahead of ourselves, though, I first want to make sure you have a clear grasp on your own call. It is imperative that you biblically frame God's call on your life—both what it means and why you should pursue it.

Lest you think I'm overhyping the grandeur of God's call, reflect with me on three key New Testament passages. In Ephesians, the apostle Paul teaches us that Christ has gifted His church, in this age, with pastors and evangelists for the work of ministry. A called minister is, quite literally, one of Christ's gifts to His church:

And He gave some as apostles, some as prophets, some as evangelists, some as pastors and teachers, for the equipping of the saints for the work of ministry, for the building up of the body of Christ; until we all attain to the unity of the faith, and of the knowledge of the Son of God, to a mature man, to the measure of the stature which belongs to the fullness of Christ. (Eph. 4:11–13)

Christ has given His church certain leaders for a certain purpose: to equip the saints for the work of ministry. But you can only pass on to others what you have received. In order to equip the saints, *you* must be equipped; in order to nurture them, *you* must be nurtured.

Moreover, in Romans, Paul unpacks God's plan to reach the nations through preachers whom He has set apart. If Ephesians 4 depicts the minister as *teaching* Christians, Romans 10 depicts the minister as *making* Christians through the preaching of the gospel. Consider Paul's airtight logic, and bask in the glory of a minister's call:

"Everyone who calls on the name of the Lord will be saved." How then are they to call on Him in whom they have not believed? How are they to believe in Him whom they have not heard? And how are they to hear without a preacher? But how are they to preach unless they are sent? Just as it is written: "How beautiful are the feet of those who bring good news of good things!" (Rom. 10:13–15)

God again makes clear that individuals are the means through which He will reconcile others to Himself (cf. 2 Cor. 5:11–21). In Paul's mind, God setting apart some for ministry is directly tethered to others becoming Christians.

> **The church has to affirm one's call to ministry. Biblically speaking, there is no such thing as a self-authenticated minister.**

In 1 Timothy, finally, Paul clarifies *who* may undertake the work of pastoral ministry. As I've mentioned, it's not a "whosoever will, may come" type of call. Your subjective desire for the work is not enough; your local church is responsible for assessing your desire and gifting. This involves together evaluating your sense of call against the objective standard of 1 Timothy 3:1–7:

It is a trustworthy statement: if any man aspires to the office of overseer, it is a fine work he desires to do. An overseer, then, must be above reproach, the husband of one wife, temperate, self-controlled, respectable, hospitable, skillful in teaching, not overindulging in wine, not a bully, but gentle, not contentious, free from the love of money. He must be one who manages his own household well, keeping his children under control with all dignity (but if a man does not know how to manage his own household, how will he take care of the church of God?), and not a new convert, so that he will not become conceited and fall into condemnation incurred by the devil. And he must have a good reputation with those outside the church, so that he will not fall into disgrace and the snare of the devil.

Do you measure up to this divine standard? Process these qualifications with your pastor(s) and church leaders. Ask them to honestly evaluate you and your desire. As I said above, the church has to affirm one's call to ministry. Biblically speaking, there is no such thing as a self-authenticated minister.

Do you see yourself in these three passages? Have you reckoned with the nobility of the work and the high qualifications for those who undertake it? This is God's view of the office you wish to hold and the service you seek to render. These are His standards for those who serve in ministry. These are His standards for you.

## ARE YOU CALLED TO MINISTRY?

So, again, is this you? Have you received a call to ministry? Do you see God at work in your life in these ways and toward these ends? Has your pastor or your elders encouraged you to pursue ministry? Has your church affirmed your calling? If questions still linger, I point you to my book *Discerning Your Call to Ministry*. It will help you engage these questions more deeply and, I hope, steer you toward greater clarity in your call.[2]

Given that this book is about succeeding at seminary, you likely believe you've received God's call and are pursuing it accordingly. That's why you're reading the book.

> **A call to ministry is a call to prepare.**

While I encourage you to settle the question of whether or not God has truly called you to ministry, don't feel pressure at this juncture to declare what type of ministry you will pursue. For some of you, that sense of calling is quite clear. You are poised to pastor, or plant a church, or serve as a student minister. You know what God has called you to do and you're eager to do it.

For others of you, your calling is clear but the specifics are not. You have a general sense God is setting you apart for a ministry of the Word, but beyond that you still have more questions than answers. That's perfectly okay, too.

Seminary is not just a season of theological formation; it's also a season of spiritual and ministerial discovery. A healthy seminary experience will not only inform the mind but shape the heart and crystallize the calling.

That's why, if you're called to ministry, a step toward seminary is a step in the right direction. A call to ministry is a call to prepare. Do your best to get the entire ministry toolkit so you are ready for whatever door God might open for you. You simply have no way of knowing what God has in store for your future.

Consider my journey in this regard, for example. In just over twenty years of ministry, I have served in roles as a student minister, assistant to the pastor, minister of outreach, college minister, pastor, interim pastor, seminary professor, seminary administrator, seminary president, and more!

Here's the point: it is impossible to predict where God will lead you, but it *is* possible to prepare for where God may lead you. That is what this book is about—your ministry preparation and how to get the most out of it.

### IN CONCLUSION

Almost every kind of invitation—yes, even to the White House—includes an RSVP date. The host needs to make appropriate preparations, and the invited guest is holding a place that could be extended to another.

Too many would-be ministers treat God's call to ministry like there is no RSVP date. They dawdle and delay, halfheartedly pursuing what's ahead. We don't send mixed signals to other invitations; why do we do so with God?

You need to operate as though you have a clear RSVP date.

Clarify your calling with your pastors and your church, seek wise counsel and helpful resources to chart your course for ministry preparation, and then, by faith, follow God's call. The needs of the church and nations are too great—and the calling to ministry too grand—to delay.

# CHAPTER 2

# Prepare for Three Years, Get Prepared for Thirty

Few men have shaped the twenty-first-century church more than John Piper, and few of his books have proven more helpful than *Brothers, We Are Not Professionals*. Piper argues that the ministry is not like other professions—such as the practice of law or medicine—but that it should be viewed as altogether different and pursued altogether differently. He writes:

> We pastors are being killed by the professionalizing of the pastoral ministry. The mentality of the professional is not the mentality of the prophet. It is not the mentality of the slave of Christ. Professionalism has nothing to do with the essence and the heart of the Christian ministry. The more professional we long to be, the more spiritual death we will leave in our wake. For there is no professional childlikeness, there is no professional tenderheartedness, there is no professional panting after God.[1]

Piper is right. Ministers shouldn't operate according to typical professional characteristics and considerations. Career trajectory, résumé building, and compensation packages shouldn't be the chief motivation. On the contrary, ministers are called to serve sacrificially and selflessly.

Yet when it comes to ministerial service, we aren't called to be amateurs either. A ministerial amateur is not one who lacks a formal credential or advanced degree from a reputable seminary; he is one who lacks the knowledge base, skill set, and focused training for faithfulness in gospel ministry. You can be an amateur even if you hold a seminary degree, and you can be a faithful minister even if you lack one.

The list of those who lacked formal theological training while affecting the world for Christ is long, and it includes luminaries such as John Bunyan, Charles Spurgeon, and Martyn Lloyd-Jones. I have personally learned much from Christians who lacked formal theological education.

However, never before in the history of the church has theological education been so accessible—and so needed. Advanced technology, innovative delivery systems, and proliferating resources all make being a ministerial amateur—as a permanent state—inexcusable.

With the previous disclaimers in mind, I encourage you to pursue formal ministry preparation at a theological institution. In the next chapter, I'll unpack what to look for in a seminary. In this chapter, though, I want to reflect with you on the importance of going to seminary in the first place.

### A TIMELESS NEED

Ministry preparation is as old as the church itself. The apostle Paul had received formal Jewish instruction at the feet of Gamaliel before receiving personal instruction from Christ Himself. Bringing this concept full circle, Paul exhorted Timothy to "be diligent to present yourself approved to God as a worker who does not need to be ashamed, accurately handling the word of truth" (2 Tim. 2:15).

Additionally, in 2 Timothy, Paul encouraged Timothy to "entrust these to faithful people who will be able to teach others also" (2 Tim. 2:2). The apostle's exhortations ring through the ages, challenging every generation of gospel ministers to be maximally prepared for ministry service. And, by the way, Timothy knew Greek, was ministerially incubated in the apostolic age, and enjoyed Paul as his personal mentor. Think about that carefully. If Timothy needed to be intentional about ministry preparation, so do you!

What's more, the defining qualification of those called to ministry is the ability to teach the Word. In fact, a close look at the qualifications for elders versus the qualifications for deacons reveals only one distinction between the two offices. The character and lifestyle qualifications are remarkably similar, but only the elder must be able to teach.

And teach the elder does. To pastor is to live in a never-ending cycle of sermon preparation and delivery. More broadly, to minister to God's people is to continually study the Word in order to preach, teach, and counsel. A call to ministry is a call to minister the Word. Thus, a call to ministry is a call to *prepare* to minister the Word.

You cannot be an effective minister without effectively ministering the Word, nor can you be a faithful minister without faithfully ministering the Word. And, at the end of the day, you'll be unable to effectively and faithfully minister the Word unless you've been effectively and faithfully *taught* it. And that, at least in our current cultural setting, typically happens at seminary.

## A DANGEROUS INCONSISTENCY

For some inexplicable reason there has often been an inconsistency between evangelicals' high view of Scripture, of the church, of gospel ministry—and our approach to ministry preparation. We take the Bible and the gospel seriously, but we're often too casual when it comes to presenting it well. Some of this tension is understandable. (*Do I delay my ministry for several years of preparation, or do I go preach Jesus now?*)

At the same time, I challenge you to treat your ministry, and the requisite preparation, with the seriousness they deserve. We apply this logic to every other area of life; why wouldn't we apply it to this most ultimate area of life?

For example, when God called me to Midwestern Seminary in 2012 and our family relocated to Kansas City, one of our first tasks was to find a new pediatrician for our five young children. We didn't look for someone who dabbled in pediatrics. We wanted a children's doctor with appropriate training, sufficient experience, and a good reputation—among other things.

Similarly, when our car needs servicing, we don't take it to a shade-tree mechanic. When we need an accountant, we don't just look for someone good with a calculator. When our favorite football team searches for a new coach, we don't want them to hire someone who's always wanted to learn more about the sport.

What's the common denominator in these examples? We insist on knowledge, training, suitable experience, and a successful track record in every meaningful area of life. The church should expect no less from its ministers. We who would minister to the church should expect no less from ourselves. And a faithful seminary will help you toward these ends.

## WHAT A HEALTHY SEMINARY PROVIDES

Of the many reasons to go to seminary, give careful attention to these nine. At seminary you will . . .

1. **Learn from gifted teachers**, all of whom are accomplished in their respective disciplines and will, most likely, be far more knowledgeable than anyone you'd have the opportunity to study with in other venues. And the relationships you develop with these mentors don't end when you graduate. You can turn to them throughout your ministry for encouragement and support.

2. **Enjoy a focused, immersive season of theological training and ministry preparation.** Life and ministry pull us toward a "Martha" way of life, but seminary forces us to focus, grow, and become more like Mary (Luke 10:38–42).

3. **Avoid gaps in your ministry preparation.** Without a structured course of study, we are inclined to read what most interests us—and avoid what does not. Seminary has a way of rounding us out, enabling us to mature into a well-informed believer with a broad-based knowledge of Scripture, theology, and ministry essentials.

4. **Cultivate humility, which is essential for Christian ministry.** Some students show up on campus thinking they know a little something, only to have their paradigms explode once they start attending lectures and reading their textbooks. Pride can flare up too, of course, but if you approach your studies with a godly mindset, you will soon realize just how much you don't know—and how much others do. Seminary incubates humility.

5. **Become better equipped to minister to a broken society and a needy church.** The twenty-first century presents societal challenges unknown to previous generations. Ethical dilemmas, moral debauchery, cultural decay, and fractured families all make ministry—in both the community and the church—increasingly complex. You need to be ready for this ministry minefield.

6. **Enjoy access to resources unavailable to you elsewhere.** In addition to the faculty and library, you will benefit from mentorship, ministry-field opportunities, conferences, workshops, and so much more. A healthy seminary is an artesian well of ministry resources and opportunities, daily giving students more than they paid for.

7. **Develop relationships that last a lifetime.** Ministry can be a lonely road. There are times we need to lean on other ministry friends who know the burdens we bear and who can, from their own experience, offer words of support. Seminary breeds such relationships.

8. **Foster self-discipline and a strong work ethic.** Though ministry preparation is not about earning a credential, a seminary degree evidences that you've taken your call to ministry seriously enough to pursue training—and that you have the self-discipline to complete it. Like it or not, churches evaluate one's ministry preparation and experience when considering a candidate. A seminary degree is a step in the right direction.

9. **Gain confidence in your ability to teach God's Word and minister to His people.** Confidence is not something you suddenly summon before your first sermon. It grows within you over time as you develop

the assurance that you've been called—and prepared—for the ministry God has set before you.

These reasons and more are why Kevin DeYoung argues: "I urge every man preparing for pastoral ministry to make every effort to go to seminary. Yes, actually go there, take classes in a building with other students, and get a degree. Again, I recognize there are exceptions to this rule. But I hope those pursuing pastoral ministry will diligently and sacrificially pursue a seminary education unless providentially hindered."[2]

### PURSUE THE MDIV DEGREE

*Where* you study is important because it determines *with whom* you will study. Again, we will unpack this more thoroughly in the next chapter. But even now, think carefully about the degree you will pursue. That will inform where you choose to study.

For many decades now, the gold-standard degree for ministry preparation has been the Master of Divinity. Regardless of the specific field in which you may serve, the MDiv is, generally speaking, the best degree to complete.

> **Completing the Master of Divinity degree doesn't ensure a faithful ministry, but it does position you for it.**

The MDiv contains the essential toolkit. You'll develop a facility with the original languages, learn the broad contours of church history, hone your ability to interpret and teach Scripture, be nurtured for Great Commission work, and get instructed in basic leadership and pastoral skills.

Completing the Master of Divinity degree doesn't ensure a faithful ministry, but it does position you for it. It's designed to prepare you for faithful service—regardless of the context in which the Lord places you. If at all possible, do not settle for anything less.

## IN CONCLUSION

The sad reality is many church members are pathetically ill-informed, but their lack of training isn't a permission slip for ministers to be the same. God does not grade ministers on the curve. We are judged by New Testament standards of scriptural knowledge and ministerial fitness, not by whether we know the Bible marginally better than poorly equipped congregants.

A call to Christian ministry is glorious, and all whom God calls must be optimally prepared to serve Him. Don't settle for the quickest or easiest degree; aim for being maximally prepared for a lifetime of faithful ministry. To do that, you need to pick the right seminary. Which leads us to chapter three.

# CHAPTER 3

# Pick the Right Institution: What to Look For and Why It Matters

As it relates to your ministry preparation, where you choose to study will prove more consequential than most any other decision you make. Countless considerations are involved; in this chapter, though, I want to focus your attention on nine questions you should ask of potential seminaries.

As you consider which seminary to attend, the stakes could hardly be higher. I well recall wrestling with this decision. I wasn't sure what I needed in a seminary, but I knew I needed the opposite of what I experienced in my undergraduate studies.

As a graduating high school student, I planned to attend college on a basketball scholarship, then enter law school, and then pursue a career accordingly. As one with many athletic-scholarship opportunities, I chose my college primarily for academic, reputational, and geographical purposes.

Yet shortly after entering college, God upended my plans. I became a Christian my freshman year and surrendered to ministry my junior year. So I plodded through my political-science degree, knowing that after graduation I was bound for seminary.

From a spiritual, theological, and worldview perspective, my undergraduate studies could hardly have been worse. My campus was the quintessential party school; it even boasted an on-campus bar. In the classroom, my religion professors undermined the Scriptures; my philosophy professors questioned the existence of God; my science professors advanced evolutionary theory; my economics professors derided free-market capitalism; and my literature professors promoted reader-response hermeneutics.

Throughout college, I had to play intellectual defense. The environment was spiritually barren; the worldview thoroughly secular. It was an altogether challenging four years.

I intuitively knew I needed the opposite for seminary. I wanted to study with professors who believed the Scriptures, who were doctrinally sound, and who would teach me a biblical worldview. I wanted to learn without having to second-guess the instructor who stood before me.

God led my wife and me to Southern Seminary in Louisville, Kentucky, where I earned MDiv and PhD degrees. While there, I enjoyed all I had hoped for and more. Now I get to lead a similar institution—one marked by doctrinal fidelity and spiritual vibrancy.

Here at Midwestern Seminary in Kansas City, Missouri, I want my students to enjoy what I experienced during my own ministry preparation and what, by God's grace, we have to offer. And I want you to be similarly selective, whether God calls you to Kansas City or to some other faithful evangelical seminary. But in

**Is the seminary positioned to undergird, not undermine, your faith?**

order to enjoy what I've been describing, you need to know what to look for.

Here are the nine must-ask questions that will help you pick the right institution:

## 1. WHAT ARE THE SEMINARY'S CONFESSIONAL COMMITMENTS?

All students should know what they can expect to be taught, and they should know it from the beginning. Does the institution have a confessional statement? If so, is it largely a formality or a functioning instrument of accountability? What does the seminary believe and teach about the Bible, the gospel, the church, marriage and gender, and the image of God? As a prospective student, does the confessional statement align with your own convictions? Is the seminary positioned to undergird, not undermine, your faith?

Midwestern Seminary is an unapologetically confessional institution, happily teaching in accordance with, and not contrary to, the *Baptist Faith and Message 2000*. Additionally, our professors ink their names to the *Chicago Statement on Biblical Inerrancy*, the *Danvers Statement on Biblical Manhood and Womanhood*, and the *Nashville Statement on Human Sexuality and Gender Roles*. Each professor must affirm these documents and teach in accordance with them. As a student, you may not affirm every point of these confessions, but it's important for you to know where your professors stand on essential matters.

## 2. WHAT IS THE SEMINARY'S PURPOSE?

Why does the seminary say it exists? Can you clearly state its calling, and does that calling resonate with yours? If you don't know why the seminary exists, it might not know either!

Every seminary worthy of consideration ought to be about the business of serving the church. John Piper encourages prospective students: "Look for a love for the church. Look for a passion to be connected with the church, not loners off doing their own academic thing, but [people who are] part of the church. . . . They want to feed the church and provide leaders for the church."[1]

I'm so committed to this conviction at Midwestern Seminary that we've adopted it formally: *For the Church*. These three words are our guiding vision, shaping each decision we make, each position we fill, each event we host, each initiative we launch, and, most definitely, each class we teach. A seminary isn't required to have *For the Church* as their official mission statement, of course, but they must be an institution precommitted to the church of the Lord Jesus Christ.

### 3. WHOM DOES THE SEMINARY SERVE?

Every seminary has a constituency—a group they look to please and under whose oversight they serve. For some seminaries, that might be an active alumni base, a generous group of donors, or some other subset of their denomination.

When you figure out who the seminary strives to serve, that will tell you a great deal about the school. It will indicate the type of faculty they will hire, the campus community they will cultivate, the events they will sponsor, and a host of other things. Ferret out whom the institution purports to serve, and how they go about that service.

### 4. HOW MUCH WILL IT COST?

In North America, the cost of higher education has skyrocketed. This is true in every field of study, including theological education. Thankfully, due to the Cooperative Program,[2] Southern Baptist seminaries remain more affordable—especially when compared to other evangelical institutions.

Yet even for institutions generously supported by their denomination, you should carefully review what they charge. What's their tuition and fee structure? What's the cost of living on or near campus? Are there hidden fees buried within their catalog? These are vital questions because they will affect how much you have to work during seminary, how quickly you can complete your degree, and the extent to which you may have to incur debt.[3]

## 5. IS THE SCHOOL SPIRITUALLY VIBRANT?

This question is difficult to answer from a distance, but it is important. Is the seminary a dry place that so prizes academic achievement that the spiritual disciplines are not championed? Is there a warmth and vibrancy to the chapel hour? Are prayer, Bible intake, worship, evangelism, and personal holiness cherished? Do you get a sense that godly professors are leading and attempting to build a God-honoring institution?

While it may be hard to ascertain answers to some of these questions, call around to local associational leaders, nearby churches, trusted alumni, and anyone else who might have insight on the school's spiritual vibrancy.

## 6. WILL THERE BE MINISTRY OPPORTUNITIES?

Every seminary worth its salt will have formal, local-church expectations for its students. Minimally, this will include active church membership. Yet students ought to desire more than this. The best ministry preparation weds classroom instruction with weekly local-church service. You should, therefore, not only look for a healthy seminary but also nearby healthy churches, where you can plug in and, perhaps, enjoy a paid ministry position.

At Midwestern Seminary, one of the ways we encourage this is with our Timothy Track program. The Timothy Track offers select residential MDiv students on-the-field ministry training in a local ministry context. Regardless of whether you're able to participate in a program like the Timothy Track, though, it is vital to gain ministry experience while completing your studies. Keep this in mind as you survey seminaries.

## 7. WHO COMPRISES THE SCHOOL'S FACULTY?

It is impossible for a seminary to rise beyond its faculty. So ask yourself: *Who teaches there? What are they known for? Will they be accessible to you? Are they willing to invest in you personally?* John Piper is right: "Don't look for a building. Don't look for a campus. Don't look for a library. Don't look for a location. Look for a faculty."[4]

This is more than a rundown of who's published what (though writing is an essential part of a faculty member's work). If theological education were merely about publications, you could just buy books, read them, and save yourself a lot of time and money. But does the faculty actually invest in students? Are internships available? Are leading professors present and accessible? Does the faculty view students as an interruption to their calling or *as* their calling?

> **It is impossible for a seminary to rise beyond its faculty. . . . Does the faculty view students as an interruption to their calling or *as* their calling?**

## 8. WHAT IS THE CAMPUS COMMUNITY LIKE?

Seminary is so much more than the formal classroom teaching. Yes, ministry preparation is taught, but it is also "caught." This takes place over coffee, in chapel, at campus events, in student housing, and in countless other venues. Is the campus community one in which you can envision yourself growing, both in Christ and in your ministry pursuit?

This is more than an assessment of amenities and events; it also entails the vibe on the ground. Is it a cheerful institution? Are the faculty, staff, and students happy to be there and encouraged about their future? Is the seminary a natural place of encouragement, organic discipleship, and group synergy about kingdom matters? Such elements should play a key role in your decision-making.

## 9. IS THE GREAT COMMISSION CELEBRATED?

Lastly, is personal evangelism and the Great Commission a box to be checked or is it an essential part of the seminary community? Does the institution long for the Lord to summon workers for the harvest? Are outreach opportunities and international mission trips front and center? Does the faculty engage in personal evangelism and let it shape their classroom instruction? Do you sense a burden for lostness, a love for the community, and a heart for the nations? If not, you will likely be served best by another seminary.

Ministry is too high a calling to enter ill-prepared, and picking a seminary is too serious a decision to make lightly. There are other considerations one should make in choosing a seminary, but these nine questions are a great place to start.

Do not enroll in a seminary without carefully considering them. Nothing short of your ministry future—and the good of Christ's church—is at stake.

# CHAPTER 4

# Online or On Campus?

Now that you have clarified where to study and what degree to pursue, the next issue for you to settle is your format of study—on campus or online?

Some educational purists lament the disruption that online education has brought, as well as the transition of theological education from solely residential to online and modular formats. I understand the frustration, but the genie is out of the bottle. Online education is here to stay. And it brings both promise and potential peril.

To be sure, the choice between online or residential education, and the seminary you choose, is interrelated. Residential studies may point you toward one seminary, whereas online may lead you in a different direction altogether. Even at this early stage in your decision-making process, though, you should determine the format of your study based on a host of personal, contextual, and ministerial circumstances.

I also know that, for many students, the choice is not binary. Many students' theological education is an amalgam of different instructional formats: on campus, online, hybrid/modular, conference classes, perhaps even a directed study or two. It may well be the same for you.

The more accurate decision, then, might be whether to be *primarily* on campus or online.

## LOSE THE STEREOTYPES

No single factor has changed higher education over the past three decades more than the advent of the internet. At the seminary level, online studies proliferated in the 2000s and came into their own in the 2010s. Over the same period of time, a stereotype arose that depicted online programs as inferior to on campus, and online students as less committed than residential ones.

> **While there are far more components to a seminary education than just knowledge, the stereotype of an inferior online education needs to be laid to rest.**

Online studies are indeed different from on campus, and in some ways they lack strengths and benefits of on campus studies. Still, data and observation have convinced me that both the student quality and learning outcomes are actually quite similar.

In fact, our seminary (and others like it) has demonstrated that when tested for information comprehension, our online students have performed equally (and occasionally slightly better) than our residential students. While there are far more components to a seminary education than just knowledge, the stereotype of an inferior online education needs to be laid to rest.

## THE PROMISE OF ONLINE EDUCATION

The promise of online education is straightforward: virtually anyone, anywhere can receive ministry preparation at any time. Such accessibility is a new reality worth celebrating. Online programs promise to unleash more seminary-trained ministers than ever before. Given the accessibility of online education, then, those who desire theological education should not hesitate to access it.

Online education often functions as either an on-ramp or an exit ramp for residential seminary training. As an on-ramp, it enables students to take classes while tidying up life's affairs before moving to seminary. As an exit ramp, it enables those called to a church before graduation to complete their degree.

> **Obedience to God's call might not include relocating to a distant city for residential theological education. In His kind providence, the online revolution means theological education can come to you when you cannot go to it.**

For other students—including those called to ministry later in life, those serving in a bivocational context, or those already enjoying a fruitful ministry—online classes enable them to gain theological training while fulfilling their current life and ministry responsibilities.

Put simply, obedience to God's call might not include relocating to a distant city for residential theological education. In His kind providence, the online revolution means theological education can come to you when you cannot go to it.

We at Midwestern Seminary were blessed to be on the cutting

edge of online education, being the first Southern Baptist seminary to offer a completely online Master of Arts degree in the late 2000s. The school remains avant-garde with our OnlineYou initiative that makes online education affordable, accessible, and customizable to the student's ministry calling.

## THE PERIL OF ONLINE EDUCATION

Like any innovation, there are concerns with online education. The most obvious entails missing out on the many upsides of residential study: life-on-life ministry preparation; profiting from chapel, campus events, and conferences; personal mentorship from professors; growing with other students in a community of learning; and being part of the *esprit de corps* (a feeling of pride, loyalty, and fellowship) of an institution. There simply is no replacement for studying on campus.

Yet there is another, less obvious, concern, which is the greatest potential downside of online education. I occasionally interact with prospective students who, though not putting it so bluntly, seem to prefer online education as a means of resisting God's call on their lives.

The scenario goes something like this. A young man believes God has called him to ministry, but he is reticent to take those initial steps of faith. Whether due to a well-paying job, the ease of living in his mother's zip code, or some other practical concern, he simply cannot get out of the boat. He wants the path of least resistance in ministry—and online education appears to be it. Almost as a tool to assuage his conscience, then, he occasionally takes an online class, sort of bumping along with no real ministry pursuit. Strangely, online education has not enabled him to follow God's call on his life; it has stymied it.

The call to ministry is a call to sacrifice for ministry. If you are not willing to sacrifice in the small things, why do you assume you'll be willing to sacrifice in the greater things? Thus, in the final analysis, the issue is not so much whether on-campus or online education is the optimum mode of study. The issue is whether you are following God's call on your life.

Whether or not the above scenario is rare in the world of online education, only time will tell. One thing I do know, however, is that God has called each of us to act in faith and not in fear. He wants us to trust Him and be willing to do hard things in His name.

> **The call to ministry is a call to sacrifice for ministry. If you are not willing to sacrifice in the small things, why do you assume you'll be willing to sacrifice in the greater things?**

Moving to a new city to attend seminary might be the scariest thing you've ever considered. If it seems far easier to stay where you are, I want to encourage you not to focus on the fear of a life change. Rather, focus on the trustworthiness and goodness of the God you serve.

### WHY ON-CAMPUS REMAINS PREFERRED

I hope it's clear by now that I am not an educational purist who laments online studies. I have fully embraced it. I even celebrate it. Nonetheless, all things being equal, I still encourage residential studies when at all possible. Here are five brief reasons why.

1. **On-campus studies enable your professors to better invest in you.** I suppose in a larger university setting, where classrooms teem with hundreds

of students, this factor is limited. But at most healthy seminaries, classes are smaller, professors are pastorally minded, and students are not just numbers. On-campus studies enable professors to more fully invest in you and you to more fully glean from them.

2. **On-campus studies enable you to benefit from the full range of on-campus activities.** Chapel, conferences, lectureships, events, and more make every week on campus a clear "value add." To be on campus is to benefit from these opportunities.

> On-campus studies enable professors to more fully invest in you and you to more fully glean from them.

3. **As I mentioned earlier, being on campus enables you to develop that *esprit de corps* with other students.** In seminary, most every student is financially strapped, struggles with Hebrew, and wrestles with issues of calling. Such circumstances enable you to encourage and be encouraged, and to struggle and overcome with other students. These shared sacrifices and experiences fortify you for the grind of ministry ahead. They also create for you ministry friends for life who will be with you for decades to come.

4. **Going to seminary brings a divine disruption to your life.** It signals to others, and to yourself, that God is calling you to ministry, and that you are following His call. If He has indeed called you to seminary, and you are resistant to that disruption, what makes you think you'd be willing to follow His call to serve a church in a new state, much less a distant mission field?

5. **You are more likely to get placed in a ministry**

**position.** Seminary administrators and faculty know residential students and are better positioned to help them. I receive requests weekly from churches and ministries looking to fill key positions. I cannot recommend students I do not know, nor can the other faculty and staff members here. Those who are out of sight are out of mind. On the contrary, those who are on campus, visible, and responsible have little difficulty finding a ministry position. Residential studies help one get placed in ministry.

> **Going to seminary brings a divine disruption to your life. It signals to others, and to yourself, that God is calling you to ministry, and that you are following His call.**

If Midwestern Seminary had a one-hundred-billion-dollar endowment, we would still happily offer online education. Our online programs are more than a source of tuition revenue; they comport with our mission to exist for the church and to train a generation of pastors, ministers, and missionaries regardless of where one lives or ministers.

Interestingly, as I write this chapter in the year 2020, the world is consumed by the COVID-19 crisis. It has brought disruption to every area of life, including theological education. We have endured shelter-in-place orders, and Midwestern Seminary and Spurgeon College—along with most every other institution in America—have transitioned most classes to online formats.

When we were forced to vacate our dormitory and transition all residential classes online, we had about six weeks left in the spring semester. In any previous generation, theological education under such circumstances would have ground to a halt. Yet given technology—and the fact that Midwestern Seminary was an early and accomplished adopter of online studies—our transition was relatively seamless.

For these reasons, and many more, I praise God for modern technology and for online education. Inasmuch as online education expedites training and broadens access, it is ripe with promise. If it becomes a pacifier, though, enabling students to skirt God's call instead of facilitating it, online education is laced with peril. Within each student, and his or her particular calling, lies the difference.

As you ponder which mode of education to pursue, ask yourself these four questions to help discern what the Lord is leading you to do:

1. Which mode of education (residential or online) do I desire the most, and why?

2. Which mode of education will best equip me to faithfully serve Christ's church?

3. Do I desire to do online education out of fear of change (or some other non-legitimate reason), or does it simply make better sense to stay in my local church or ministry?

4. Is there a community in my current local church that I can trust to help me grow and hold me accountable throughout my seminary education?

I hope that after reading this chapter and pondering these questions, you have a greater sense of how you should pursue your seminary education. Let's now turn to an imperative aspect of your ministry calling, and therefore a key point of emphasis for your seminary success.

# CHAPTER 5

# Guard Your Life and Your Doctrine

It has now been some twenty years since my wife, Karen, and I moved from Mobile, Alabama, to Louisville, Kentucky, for my seminary training. We were in Louisville for eleven years as I completed two degrees, pastored two churches, and served in several different roles at Southern Seminary.

During those eleven years, we also had five children and went from being newlyweds to an established family (minivan and all). Throughout our years in the Louisville area, we drove home to Mobile about three times yearly. This typically included a beach vacation in the summer, another trip around the holidays, and another for a wedding, funeral, or some other special occasion.

As we drove the straight shot up and down I-65 scores of times, we developed our own peculiar travel habits along the way. We tried not to stop if the children were sleeping, tried to see how long we could travel between stops, and tried to see how quickly we could make the trip overall.

As you can imagine, we gained a keen familiarity with the 630-mile route. We knew where the best rest stops were, which exits had a Chick-fil-A or Starbucks, and which service stations were ideal.

We always made mental calculations: *If we don't stop now, it will be another ninety miles before we come to an exit we like.* So we learned to take the right exit ramps, at the right times, knowing the best ones were few and far between.

I tell you this because, in a similar fashion, we all move briskly down the highway of life. We travel pedal to the metal, ingraining bad habits and unideal life patterns along the way. As years become decades, we wish for do-overs, for the chance to choose differently.

Life presents very few exit ramps that prompt us to pull over, reflect, and recalibrate our priorities and patterns. For some, it is a critical illness; for others, the death of a loved one; for others, a job loss or an excruciating ministry season.

If you are pursuing ministry, seminary can be one such defining off-ramp. Indeed, it must be.

## SEMINARY, A DIVINE DISRUPTION

As we've seen, attending seminary is a major threshold to cross. Taking that step typically means you believe you're called to ministry, a church has affirmed that calling, and an admissions committee has looked favorably on your personal and academic information.

Most everything about seminary is disruptive: often it means a new city with new employment, new housing, new friends, a new church, and new needs and opportunities.

Even if you don't move to become a residential student, the disruption is still real. Immersing yourself in studies will affect every area of life, including work, family, ministry, and recreation. Seminary is a divine disruption—and that can be a good thing.

Seminary invites us—demands us—to take stock of our lives. Sinful habits, if we let them persist, will eventually stymie or shipwreck our ministry. During seminary, then, we work to cultivate greater self-discipline, fervency in prayer, deepening holiness, and sacrificial love for Christ and His church.

> **Immersing yourself in studies will affect every area of life, including work, family, ministry, and recreation. Seminary is a divine disruption—and that can be a good thing.**

In short, I am asking you to consider how the "off-ramp" of seminary can be a crucial juncture to reflect on what you believe, why you believe it, and how that affects everything else in your life. This process must not be taken lightly; indeed, guard it with all the mental energy and spiritual vigor you have.

### GUARD YOUR LIFE AND YOUR DOCTRINE

Perhaps more than any other New Testament verse, 1 Timothy 4:16 arrives with both warning and promise for the ministry. The warning is more implicit; the promise is unmistakably explicit. Paul writes to Timothy: "Pay close attention to yourself and to the teaching; persevere in these things, for as you do this you will save both yourself and those who hear you."

Note carefully the truth contained here. Implicitly, if we are careless with our doctrine or our living, our soul—and the souls of those to whom we minister—are endangered. How is this the case? If our lives or doctrine are off, we will prove an untrue guide for the sheep. We will invariably point them off course, leading them away from the Chief Shepherd.

Yet this warning is also pregnant with promise. As we guard our lives and doctrine, we ensure salvation for ourselves and those to whom we minister. Sound doctrine and sound living indicate we are authentic followers of Christ. They indicate a steady guide who leads the sheep toward, not away from, Him.

While in seminary, much time will be devoted to your doctrine. It is a time of doctrinal formation—and that is a good thing. A seminary that does not prioritize your theological formation is not worthy of your tuition.

If you are not careful, though, an imbalance can develop. Books commenting on Scripture can replace the reading of Scripture itself. Paper writing can dry up your prayer life. Exercises for ministry formation can supplant actual, hands-on ministry. In other words, your doctrine can flourish while your spiritual life flounders.

> **A seminary that does not prioritize your theological formation is not worthy of your tuition.**

In his must-read book *Exegetical Fallacies*,[1] D. A. Carson comments on this phenomenon by telling the story of one "Ernest Christian." Ernest was converted in high school, was deeply involved in his college ministry, was growing immensely in Bible study and prayer, and sensed a call to vocational ministry. After being affirmed by his church, he moved off to be trained at seminary. Carson continues:

After Ernest has been six months in seminary, the picture is very different. Ernest is spending many hours a day memorizing Greek morphology and learning the details of the itinerary of Paul's second missionary journey. Ernest has also begun to write exegetical papers; but by the time he has finished his lexical study, his syntactical diagram, his survey of critical opinions, and his evaluation of conflicting evidence, somehow the Bible does not feel as alive to him as it once did. Ernest is troubled by this; he finds it more difficult to pray and witness then he did before he came to seminary.[2]

Anyone familiar with seminary life knows this story is too often true. Students arrive "bright eyed and bushy tailed," ready to conquer the world for Jesus. They get immersed in academic work and theological debate—only to one day realize they have left their first love (Rev. 2:1–7) and forgotten why they are even at seminary to begin with.

This doesn't have to be the case! There is a better way. Remember the apostle's dual emphasis in 1 Timothy 4:16, and stubbornly guard both life and doctrine as you learn and grow.

In truth, we must not choose between love of God and love of doctrine; it is not an "either/or" but a "both/and." How do you truly love someone you don't really know? The great Presbyterian theologian B. B. Warfield underscores this point:

Sometimes we hear it said that ten minutes on your knees will give you a truer, deeper, more operative knowledge of God than ten hours over your books. "What!" is the appropriate response. "Than ten hours over your books *on* your knees?" Why should you turn from God when you turn to your books, or feel that you must turn from your books in order to turn to God? If learning and devotion are as antagonistic as that, then the intellectual life is in itself accursed and there can be no question of a religious life for a student, even of theology.[3]

The heart posture with which you pursue your education will make all the difference in the world. Reject a dry, stuffy faith built on knowledge alone; choose instead a thoughtful, deepening faith built on truth and love.

### KEYS TO GUARDING YOUR LIFE IN SEMINARY

In light of this danger, here is some practical wisdom that has proved helpful to me over the years. Consider five keys by which you can guard your life in seminary:

1. **Cultivate the spiritual disciplines.** The spiritual disciplines remain the lifeblood for every believer. Prayer, worship, Bible intake, journaling, and others are essential for a growing follower of Christ—regardless of age or season of life. Forge these in seminary and prioritize them day by day. They will carry you through seminary and propel you forward for a lifetime of ministry.[4]

2. **Establish healthy habits.** Habits are easy to make and hard to break—bad habits at least. Good habits, meanwhile, require intentionality on the front end but can provide a lifetime of structure and reinforcing practices. Set your rhythms accordingly: awaken early, read your Bible before textbooks, commune with God before conversing with others, integrate fasting, pray with your spouse before going to bed, and so on.

3. **Prioritize prayer.** As a nonquantifiable discipline, prayer is easy to gloss over. We *know* when we've read three chapters of Scripture; we may not be as aware when we've rushed through our prayer time. So keep a prayer list and a prayer journal. Tracking what you need to pray for will bring added motivation. Documenting God's answers will inspire you all the more.

4. **Think devotionally about your studies.** While some professors will draw the lines from their lectures

to your spiritual formation, others will not. But you can draw them. Ask yourself questions like, *What can I apply from this reading to my spiritual life? What sin does this lecture prompt me to confess? How will this assignment strengthen me for ministry in the local church? What new truth about God did I learn today?* As you learn to ask the right questions, you will find yourself getting more out of seminary, spiritually speaking, than you ever imagined.

**5. Look for Jesus in all.** Jesus is the apex of Scripture; therefore He should be the apex of your studies. Listen for Him in every lecture. Look for Him in every reading. Ask your professor how a given biblical passage connects to Him. For additional reading on this topic, I recommend *How to Stay Christian in Seminary* by David Mathis and Jonathan Parnell.[5]

> **As you learn to ask the right questions, you will find yourself getting more out of seminary, spiritually speaking, than you ever imagined.**

At the beginning of this chapter, I mentioned our move to Louisville for seminary training. That was early August 2001. Thankfully, for the three years prior, I served under Dr. Steve Lawson at Dauphin Way Baptist Church. Dr. Lawson was a pivotal influence on my life. He became not only a mentor but a dear friend and remains one to this day.

Dr. Lawson always took interest in young men called to ministry, and there were a number of them in our church. But I sensed he took a particular interest in me. One day I asked why. He reflected, "If a man has $100 to invest in a business, he wants to invest it in the business that will bring the greatest return. I am investing in you because I believe you will bring a return for the kingdom. Make sure you do just that."

Dr. Lawson's words inspired me then—and they still do. They convicted me then—and they still do. Such words remind me that my ministry is a stewardship—and so is yours.

Many have invested much in you. God has called you. Christ has strengthened you. The Holy Spirit has gifted you. Churches have supported you. Pastors have mentored you. Family members have sacrificed for you. Benefactors have invested in you. Professors have taught you. Fellow students have encouraged you.

You are a steward of a precious call, and so many others are invested in it with you. Therefore, you must guard your life and your doctrine. And seminary is one of the best places to establish healthy patterns to enable you to do just that.

# CHAPTER 6

# Steward Your Time—It's Your Most Valuable Asset

Many of you reading this book have ambled through life without much focus or self-discipline. You've made suitable grades in school, held down a job sufficient to meet your needs, and, without too much exertion, fulfilled family and ministry commitments. Life has been full but manageable. Yet before you now stands seminary, and something within you beckons for more.

That's basically my story. Though always insatiably curious, in high school I was an athlete first. I made suitable grades but would not have been called a bookworm. In college, I took my studies more seriously, but as my passions moved toward ministry, so did my reading habits. In seminary, I knew I was, alas, in God's will and pursuing His calling. I wanted to excel academically. But it didn't just happen. I had to be intentional about stewarding my time.

## STEWARDING TIME IS ESSENTIAL

Seminary tends to be the season where responsibilities and opportunities—each in growing numbers—collide and squeeze you in the middle. I realize the typical seminary student is nontypical. Seminaries draw different people from different backgrounds, life stages, and circumstances. Yet for many, seminary is when you are thrown into a spiraling vortex of busyness.

Your program of study will likely be the most rigorous academic effort you've ever undertaken. And unlike college, you may also have family and work responsibilities. You are studying for ministry, and so you should be engaged in ministry, too. You will discover sermon preparation can be a bottomless pit of exegetical digging. You will develop new friendships, and those take time. On top of all that, you will have the nagging sense you should be more disciplined in prayer, Bible study, and personal evangelism. Which, of course, requires significant time as well.

I have learned that life tends to get fuller and busier with each passing year. Like barnacles, you accumulate more responsibilities and opportunities year by year—and these can become all-encompassing, choking out discretionary time. Needless to say, many seminarians simply drown.

You will too if you don't steward your time wisely.

## STEWARDING TIME IS A BIBLICAL MANDATE

We must remember that stewarding time wisely isn't just a matter of time management or life hacks; it is a kingdom priority. Consider Ephesians 5:15–16: "So then, be careful how you walk, not as unwise people but as wise, making the most of your time, because the days are evil."

Paul is calling us to be mindful of how we conduct our everyday lives. He summons us to be wise walkers, and then clarifies the how: by making the most of our time. Commentator Peter O'Brien helpfully notes:

The verb "redeem" is drawn from the commercial language of the marketplace, and its prefix denotes an intensive activity, a buying which exhausts the possibilities available. It seems better, then, to understand the expression as metaphorical, signifying to "make the most of the time." *Believers will act wisely by snapping up every opportunity that comes.*[1]

That last sentence is a tight paraphrase that captures Paul's sentiment. We are to use our time to advance the cause of Christ.

Additionally, note Paul's reason for redeeming the time—"because the days are evil." Maximizing our time is hard enough, but we also have a real adversary who opposes us. O'Brien's comments are again helpful:

The notion that "the days are evil" appears to be similar to the idea of "this present evil age" in Galatians 1:4 (cf. "the *evil* day," Eph. 6:13). These "evil" days are under the control of the prince of the power of the air (Eph. 2:2), who is opposed to God and his purposes. He exercises effective and compelling authority over men and women outside of Christ, keeping them in terrible bondage (2:1–3). But the Ephesian Christians have already participated in the world to come, the powers of the new age have broken in upon them, and they have become "light in the Lord" (5:8). Although they live in the midst of these evil days as they await their final redemption, they are neither to avoid them nor to fear them. Rather, they are to live wisely, taking advantage of every opportunity in this fallen world to conduct themselves in a manner that is pleasing to God.[2]

We, just like the ancient Ephesians, live in an evil age. And like them, we also engage this age through Christ. He has redeemed us and given us a new lens through which we now see the world.

### KEYS TO STEWARDING TIME IN SEMINARY

Before moving to the practical, note one additional upside of stewarding your time wisely: your newfound focus doesn't just enable you to maximize your studies; it sets you on course for long-term faithfulness and healthier life rhythms.

You see, seminary studies make you a better minister not just because of what you learn, but because of the maturity, responsibility, and self-discipline the entire process cultivates. Here are five keys that will help you steward your time wisely while in seminary:

1. **Envision your ministry in light of eternity.** We've already considered Ephesians 5:16, but consider also John 9:4, where Jesus instructs His disciples: "We must carry out the works of Him who sent Me as long as it is day; night is coming, when no one can work." An eternal perspective really does reframe your ministry—and your preparation for it. You are studying not to earthly ends but heavenly ones. So make your time count.

2. **Keep your roles and goals ever before you.** Stephen Covey popularized the roles-and-goals matrix,[3] which I have now employed for years. Your *roles* include the divinely ordained positions God has given you. These may include disciple, minister, student, spouse, parent, employee, and so on. Since these roles are divinely given, and therefore meaningful, you should associate *goals* with them—progress you want to see,

things you want to achieve. Being clear about roles and goals will simplify your life and will be a strategic step toward better stewarding your time.

3. **Prioritize your life, then allocate time backward.** Now that you have clarified your roles and goals, work backward to allocate your time accordingly. John Maxwell has quipped that budgeting is "telling your money where to go instead of wondering where it went."[4] Your time is similar. Tell it where to go before it's up and gone. And as you work backward, you can prayerfully and strategically allocate it in ways that best honor God, acknowledge life's realities, and precommit you to spend time on what matters most.

Even more practically, set a concrete schedule for your day. Let's say you're a married student who must work a full-time job during seminary in order to support your family. On average, most seminarians need at least two hours every day for coursework. So, for studies not to kill family time, I suggest either waking up two hours earlier in the morning or staying up two hours later in the evening. This is

> **While seminary is a sacrifice, make sure your family is not what's actually being sacrificed.**

a minimal sacrifice you can make, and it will certainly help your family feel more loved and cared for.

While seminary is a sacrifice, make sure your family is not what's actually being sacrificed. As long as you're willing to give up a little sleep or "me" time, you should be able to master your schedule without letting it master you.

4. **Think before saying "yes."** It's cliché but true: to say yes to one thing is to say no to something else. Many overcommit because they're reluctant to disappoint, especially in person. Never feel pressure to make a commitment on the spot. Let people know you need to review the opportunity with your calendar and the appropriate stakeholders, perhaps your elders or your spouse. Say with integrity, "If my schedule permits, I would be delighted to do so." This gives you space to review the invitation with a clear head and more objective data. Never commit on the spot.

5. **Use your entire toolkit.** In God's kind providence, modern technology presents us with a significant toolkit for managing our lives—in time, stewardship, and efficiency. I use my online calendar for appointments and Evernote for responsibilities and tasks. (At the top of my Evernote task page, I list my roles with their respective goals.) Additionally, I use tools like email, text messaging, Zoom, Skype, and social media to connect with others. I encourage you to do the same.

As mentioned previously, I'm writing this book during the onslaught of COVID-19. It has upended our lives—and our plans. As I type, we're in the middle of a multiweek national shutdown. Travel has all but ceased. The vast majority of businesses are closed. Schools and institutions have moved classes online. Most sports—from professional to little league—have suspended their seasons. Extracurricular activities have been canceled. Our lives have come to a screeching halt.

*My* life has been upended, too. Days at the seminary have been long as I've had to adapt and lead. But evenings have been blessedly simple and unexpectedly sweet. All of my travel has been canceled, as have all of our children's activities. Thus, we've been home together, night after night, week after week. And honestly, I have loved every minute of it. (Okay, most minutes of it.)

This divine interruption has brought our family closer together and closer to the Lord. We've enjoyed extended conversations, lengthy family meals, and an abundance of games and activities. All of this has prompted me to resolve not to resume my pre-coronavirus schedule with all the hectic travel and evening responsibilities it entailed.

For me, it took a global pandemic to reevaluate my commitments and to, yet again, resolve to steward my time more wisely. Let me encourage you to think through this process as well, which leads to another important aspect of seminary: managing your home life while accomplishing your studies.

# CHAPTER 7

# Get an A at Home, Even if It Means a C in Class

Before entering my first pastorate, I prayed the Lord would make it a healthy ministry experience for me—and for my wife. Intuitively, I sensed this first pastorate would be trajectory-setting, propelling me down the ministry road for better or for worse. It would also likely shape our view of the church and our commitment to serving it long term.

Looking back now, I should have taken my prayer farther upstream. I should have been more concerned with my wife enjoying a healthy *seminary* experience, not just a healthy first pastorate. By God's grace we had a healthy seminary experience, but it was more accidental than intentional on my part. My wife, and our entire family, look back with fondness on our years of ministry preparation.

You can too, but you will likely need to be more intentional than I was to ensure it.

## GET AN A AT HOME

I once heard Danny Akin exhort students to "get an A at home, even if it means a C in class. It is better than getting a C at home and an A in class." I was one of those students, in fact, sitting in new-student orientation. His words landed on my heart with the ring of wisdom and truth.

I now offer similar words during new-student orientations at Midwestern Seminary. I see students—and their spouses—nod in agreement as I offer this advice. And they should. It is an essential word of counsel for seminarians.

You likely know the priority Scripture places on the family; you are acquainted with its model for a Christ-honoring home. It's not complicated: you can have a healthy family without having a healthy ministry, but you cannot have a healthy ministry without having a healthy family. Which means that prioritizing your family *is* prioritizing your ministry.

### REFLECTING ON THE MINISTER'S FAMILY LIFE

As we have seen, one's family life is central in Paul's list of ministry qualifications. In 1 Timothy 3:4–5, he writes, "He must be one who manages his own household well, keeping his children under control with all dignity (but if a man does not know how to manage his own household, how will he take care of the church of God?)."

Paul uses a lesser-to-greater argument to emphasize his point. How can you expect to effectively lead and shepherd God's church if you cannot effectively lead your own family? Or, as theologian Robert Yarbrough puts it, "If he fails here [at home], what hope does he have for overseeing an entire congregation made up of many families plus others?"[1] Shepherding your family well in seminary is preparation for shepherding them well in full-time ministry. It will be essential then; it is essential now.

Realize that throughout your seminary training (and throughout your ministry), your family's needs will be a moving target. For me, seminary grew increasingly complex on the family front. My wife and I moved to campus in 2001 with no children; by 2008, while in the throes of my PhD program, we had five.

Of course they were happily received additions, but each new child brought its own wrinkle of complexity. It was imperative for us, and it will be imperative for you, to know your particular life stage. If you are attentive to where you are as a family, you can wisely plan for the assorted complications thrown your way.

In other words, you'll need to learn the art of how to winsomely *adjust*. New responsibilities and challenges will arise that are simply unpredictable. The big question is, how will you respond? Handling tough situations in a Christlike manner takes maturity and patience, yes, but some intentionality and awareness go a long way, too.

Additionally, you don't want to unwittingly foster a critical attitude in your family toward the church or your ministry preparation. If your family feels displaced due to your studies or ministry concerns, a subtle grievance might grow and prove to be a spiritual hindrance. Central to leading your family well is instilling in them a sense of the attractiveness of Christ and the joy of serving His church. If your family feels second to the church, they may resent the very person you left everything to follow (Luke 5:11) and His church for which He died.

Tragically, some ministers disqualify themselves because of how they treat their families. Please don't let that be you. If you can create healthy family patterns now during your seminary years, it will serve you far more than you can imagine when you are on the front lines.

**EXCELLING IN THE HOME AND THE CLASSROOM**

But here's the good news: most students *can* excel both in the home and in the classroom. Consider six keys to that end:

1. **Remember that both your studies and your family are arenas to honor God.** All of life is to be lived for God's glory, and both family and ministry preparation are unique venues for this to happen. As you undertake these with spiritual mindedness, biblical wisdom, strategic time allocation, and mature prioritization, you can honor God in both without compromising either. Set out to do just that.

2. **Ensure your spouse benefits from seminary, too.** A strong seminary will seek to minister not just to the student but to his or her family as well. Perhaps your spouse desires to earn a degree or take classes along with you. Labor to make that happen. At Midwestern Seminary, my wife leads the Midwestern Women's Institute (MWI), which "is a residential certificate program that exists to equip women to serve their families, churches, and communities by providing them with ministry training, spiritual encouragement, and biblical fellowship."[2]

   I am grateful for how MWI engages the women on our campus, and I consistently hear how the program blesses the wives of our male students. Thus, I strongly encourage our male students to support their wives in this endeavor.

   Involve your spouse in your studies as well. Ask for help proofreading a theology paper. Enlist them to quiz you on names and dates in church history. Share what you are learning in exegesis class. The more seminary is about the two of you learning together, the more enjoyable it will be for both of you.

3. **Cultivate friends as couples.** In seminary, you will likely make friends for life. That was true for us; I developed a few close guy friends and my wife a few close girlfriends. But the most encouraging and lasting friendships we developed were with other couples. These relationships have been life-giving. In the midst of intense study, your family needs to be around others with whom you all can relate and relax. And since these couples are walking through many of the same pressures and difficulties, they will be able to offer timely advice and friendship. With the advances of modern technology, it's easier than ever to stay in touch with and receive continual support from such friends—even when ministry assignments have separated you by hundreds of miles.

> **The more seminary is about the two of you learning together, the more enjoyable it will be for both of you.**

4. **Seize seminary-community opportunities.** Prioritize seminary-sponsored events and gatherings. Attend the fall festival and the spring picnic. Go to chapel as a family. At Midwestern Seminary, we provide free childcare for couples who want to attend chapel together but whose kids are too young to enjoy the hour. The more seminary includes the entire family, the easier it will be to sustain family-wide joy while there. As you get the whole family involved in campus events, you can instill a sense of belonging that will leave fond memories for years to come.

5. **Commit to having less "me time."** The truth of the matter is, getting an A at home and a C in class—as opposed to a C at home and an A in class—is often a false choice. Most students can excel at both. As we saw in the last chapter, though, it takes careful time-management and focused self-discipline—which likely translates into longer days and shorter nights. Again, prioritize engagement with your family during daytime hours and give yourself to your studies before they wake up or after they go to sleep.

6. **Move through your studies.** Lastly, plot your academic course and plow through it as quickly, albeit responsibly, as possible. Your studies will likely wear on your spouse even more than they wear on you—especially if your spouse is working long hours to support you. So involve your spouse in your course selection, inform him or her of your time horizon, and keep him or her apprised of the progress you're making. I'll never forget my wife's sense of relief when I completed my PhD. I grew to learn that my academic work weighed on her as much as it did me—and the sense of accomplishment that graduation brought was not personal; it was mutual.

Your ministry preparation is a precious stewardship, but your family is more so. Put them first—and don't blame them if you underachieve at school. Most students can excel in both categories; resolve to be such a student. Let me conclude by leaving you with this challenging quote from the Puritan Matthew Henry. Read it carefully. Chew on every word. Then apply it to your family:

> **Your ministry preparation is a precious stewardship, but your family is more so.**

If therefore our houses be houses of the Lord, we shall for that reason love home, reckoning our daily devotion the sweetest of our daily delights; and our family-worship the most valuable of our family-comforts. . . . A church in the house will be a good legacy, nay, it will be a good inheritance, to be left to your children after you.[3]

May this be your goal. Regardless of how busy you become in the midst of your studies, remember your primary call to shepherd your family. If, at the end of your studies, you achieve a degree but lose your family in the process, you have experienced a net loss. But if you get your degree and nurture your family in the process, you will have much to rejoice about, together, on graduation day. Pray and strive for the latter scenario. You will not regret it.

# CHAPTER 8

# Plan Your Finances

When my wife and I moved to seminary in the summer of 2001, we arrived with little money but no debt. On the front end I had lined up a part-time job at the seminary, and my wife a full-time job. Together, we made about $2,000 per month. We were certainly not living large, but we had a plan and were positioned to navigate our way through. Along the way, however, I experienced something that far outstripped our plan—God's kind providence. Follow the story with me.

As we prepared for our move to seminary, my home church gave us a generous cash gift, as did several church members. Upon arriving in Louisville, the Lord sent us many blessings— preaching opportunities, unexpected checks from friends and family, and grants from both the Alabama Baptist Convention and the Kentucky Baptist Convention. What is more, we were blessed by Guidestone Financial Resources' seminary-student insurance plan. We found ourselves not with more money than we could imagine but certainly with more than we expected.

By year two of my MDiv degree, I'd entered my first pastorate. My church generously cared for us and individual members additionally so. Though I never solicited donations for seminary, generous friends, kindhearted congregants, and loving family members continually surprised us. Or, better stated, God continued to surprise us.

Every step of the way, He provided everything we needed. I completed two seminary degrees without incurring any debt and without my family enduring financial hardship along the way. The point of sharing my journey is not for you to marvel at my accomplishment, but for you to marvel at God's provision. Nor do I want to minimize any financial hardship you may experience during seminary; I simply want to challenge you not to underestimate God's provision along the way.

If He has called you to ministry, He is calling you to prepare. Surely He will not abandon you as you pursue Him. While my experience may not be standard, I am confident far too many delay seminary because of *potential* financial difficulties—without ever really exhausting the opportunities available. They rightly recognize the uncertainty involved in moving to a new place, finding a new job, and incurring new expenses, but they don't pursue solutions to these challenges. Part of my aim in this chapter is to convince you that God has faithfully provided for students in the past, and He's still doing the very same thing today.

## TUITION MATTERS

The primary financial cost, of course, will be tuition and fees. I keep my finger on the pulse of costs in higher education, and especially in theological education. Frankly, I am shocked by the staggering prices charged by many schools, including theological ones.

Thankfully, as a Southern Baptist institution, Midwestern Seminary students are generously subsidized through the Cooperative Program (as are other Southern Baptist seminary students). On average, then, tuition for Southern Baptist

Convention (SBC) students is about 50 percent of what they would pay at a non-SBC institution. This reduced tuition is possible thanks to the generous contributions of SBC churches to the Cooperative Program.

In general, the world of higher education finds schools playing two games with tuition. The first is "discounting," where virtually no one pays the listed, high sticker price; each student enters into what amounts to be a personalized negotiation. Think of it like buying an automobile from a car lot. Every vehicle has a listed price, but only a sucker pays it.

The other game takes the opposite angle. The institution lists a lower tuition price, which looks attractive until the student discovers hidden fees along the way. To be clear, seminaries must charge tuition and fees—and strong institutions more so, in order to recruit and retain top-notch faculty, as well as provide other amenities and services to students.

For you, the student, please use discernment. It is right to think critically about tuition, to seek clarity on price points, and to weigh it all in terms of financial and ministry stewardship. As I've said before, you will ultimately be held accountable for how you steward all God has entrusted to you. This includes wise decisions about how to spend your money on seminary training.

At Midwestern Seminary, we believe affordability is missiologically important. High tuition discourages students, delays their course of study, and may well hinder their kingdom service after graduation. Like every other institution, we have bills to pay, and we are strategic with our resources. Students should be strategic with theirs.

### CRAFT YOUR PLAN

The most important step for you to take is putting a plan on paper. Ferret out expenses, actual and potential. Clarify income streams. Seek out grants and other sources of support. The plan matters, but the process of planning even more so.

It was Jesus, after all, who asked: "For which one of you, when he wants to build a tower, does not first sit down and calculate the cost, to see if he has enough to complete it?" (Luke 14:28). Use intentionality as you craft your financial plan for seminary, shaping it in light of the following factors and goals.

1. **Clarify the cost of your studies.** A host of factors go into this calculation, including tuition and fees based on the degree you will pursue and the institution at which you will study. You'll also want to access support materials such as books, laptops, and so on. If you're moving to campus, you'll want a general sense of the cost of living, especially housing.

2. **Get your financial house in order.** If you haven't developed the discipline of budgeting, now is the time. If you are not well informed about personal finance in general, grab a resource by someone like Dave Ramsey,[1] Art Rainer,[2] or Larry Burkett.[3] On the front end, eliminate all unnecessary expenses. Resolve to live thin for a few years. Those who enter seminary in a healthy financial position are more likely to graduate in the same.

> **Those who enter seminary in a healthy financial position are more likely to graduate in the same.**

3. **Purpose to avoid debt.** Avoiding debt may be unrealistic for some, but I want to encourage you to strive to complete your studies debt-free. Accrued debt can become a ministerial headwind,

limiting where and under what circumstances you can serve in the future. Some mission agencies will not send you overseas if you have personal indebtedness. Again, some may find student-loan debt unavoidable; I fully understand. But do your best to limit it as much as possible, borrowing only as truly necessary.

4. **Make your needs known.** God's people are generous, but they need to know of individual needs. By this I don't mean announcing, "We need $600 by the end of the month to pay our rent." Prior to that point, let your church know you plan to attend seminary. Ask your pastor if he can share that with the congregation, pray for you, and let them know of the financial costs. You'll be amazed by God's provision through His people.

5. **Shake every known tree.** Craft an e-newsletter you can periodically send to friends and families to update them on your studies and needs. Meet with a financial-aid advisor at your desired institution about scholarships and on-campus employment. Again, let your church and other churches know you are pursuing seminary. Explore grant opportunities. Inquire at your workplace about tuition-reimbursement benefits, or perhaps take a job that offers such. Reach out to your denomination's associational and state-convention offices for seminary grants. Finally, if your income is low enough, you may qualify for government assistance. There's no shame in that. For a season, we qualified for government assistance, and it was a huge source of help to us.

6. **Be willing to embrace a different lifestyle for a few years.** Perhaps you already have a good job, a nice house, and live a pretty comfortable life. Your call to ministry has seemingly upended your version of the

"American Dream." You want to be faithful to the Lord's call, but you are having a hard time processing actually giving up what you've worked so hard to achieve.

If that's you, recognize the biblical imperative to follow Jesus wherever He leads, regardless of cost (Matt. 16:24–27). Faithfulness to His calling will be far more rewarding than material accumulation. And these short few years of training will have a far greater impact on your life—and the lives of others—than optimizing your earning potential.

Though it may appear that you're going *backward* by taking a pay cut, embracing uncertainty, and moving to a new place for a few years, in the grand scheme of things you are actually moving *forward* in faithfulness and dependence on the Lord.

In over twenty years of studying and serving in seminary contexts, I've never known a student who moved to campus only to soon return home due to finances. I've known many who had to sacrifice to make it through, and a few we might even classify as having suffered in the process, but I know none who simply *had* to abandon their calling.

As you plan your finances, don't wait until everything looks optimal. That day may never come. To put it another way, attending seminary is like having your first child. If you wait until all the circumstances seem perfect and you're in a dream financial position, you'll never start a family—or attend seminary either.

# CHAPTER 9

# Hit the Books

You are pursuing theological education because you believe God has called you to ministry, and you sense the need to prepare. When it comes to this preparation, one of your primary tools will be books. Lots of them.

You'll encounter books on preaching, exegesis, ethics, apologetics, church history, Greek, Hebrew, and on and on—but don't miss their purpose. They exist to prepare you to equip the saints for the work of ministry (Eph. 4:11–16).

You'll have to navigate unimaginable scenarios and unanticipated challenges in ministry. Some challenges will be spiritual, theological, or ethical; others may be cultural, financial, interpersonal, or logistical. Given our rapidly changing world, altogether unforeseen challenges will no doubt appear on the horizon.

Your seminary training will equip you for many of these conundrums—but not all. It should, however, equip you to *search* for and *find* answers to such challenges. In other words, both your course of study itself, and the discipline of study you develop, will position you for ministry faithfulness.

Some of you are natural students. You've long practiced good study habits, and seminary will be no different. But

**Given the grandeur of your calling, the complexity of our times, the needs of the church, and the richness of Scripture, you'll want to hit the books as never before.**

that's not the case for others of you. Seminary will be the most rigorous academic experience of your life, and you'll have to quickly up your game.

In either case, seminary is a new beginning. Given the grandeur of your calling, the complexity of our times, the needs of the church, and the richness of Scripture, you'll want to hit the books as never before.

## STUDY: A BIBLICAL COMMITMENT

On occasion I encounter someone who believes study, and especially formal theological training, is unnecessary if not downright unspiritual. As we saw earlier, while ministry *preparation* is nonnegotiable, a formal seminary degree is not a prerequisite for ministry service. God has and will use many non-credentialed ministers in spectacular ways for His own glory. He's done so in my life and probably in yours, too.

And yet ministry preparation is essential, and regular study—even post-graduation—is a biblical command. The apostle Paul cited the ongoing ability to teach as an essential ministerial qualification. Thus, he challenged Timothy: "Be diligent to present yourself approved to God as a worker who does not need to be ashamed, accurately handling the word of truth" (2 Tim. 2:15). Donald Guthrie, commenting on this verse, helpfully says:

> The shame that any workman feels when the incompetence or shoddiness of his work is detected is used as a figure

for the Christian ministry. *A workman who does not need to be ashamed* must, therefore, be understood in the sense of a Christian teacher who can unblushingly submit his work for God's approval, like the men in the parable of the talents who had gained other talents. This unashamedness is achieved when the workman *correctly handles the word of truth*.[1]

The ability to "unblushingly submit one's work to God for His approval" doesn't just happen, though. Correctly handling Scripture takes diligent work, deep thinking, and dogged perseverance. Superficial readers and preachers *of* the Word re-create superficial believers *in* the Word. Regrettably for many of us, laziness in study is a besetting sin. R. C. Sproul confirms this:

Here then is the real problem of our negligence. We fail in our duty to study God's Word not so much because it is difficult to understand, not so much because it is dull and boring, but because it is work. Our problem is not a lack of intelligence or a lack of passion. Our problem is that we are lazy.[2]

If you aren't given to study, then pastoral ministry may simply not be for you. No matter what, though, let the above serve as a gentle prod when laziness begins to knock on your door. Consider the toil of studying as something like an investment. The more you put in early and often, the more return you will enjoy in the years to come.

**Superficial readers and preachers of the Word re-create superficial believers in the Word.**

## HOW TO OPTIMIZE YOUR STUDIES

The reality is, you will devote too much time and money *not* to optimize your studies. Seminary is a unique and singular window of time when others will invest in you—and you in yourself—to prepare for a lifetime of fruitful service. Get the most out of it! Here are nine ways to do just that:

1. **Keep your priorities straight.** This happens as you remember why you entered seminary in the first place. Your calling to ministry is, aside from your salvation, the highest calling of all; therefore it deserves your best efforts.

   To this end, track your syllabus expectations and assignments daily. Allocate sufficient time to complete each assignment. Make a reading plan by dividing the number of pages you must read (all your books for the semester combined) by the number of days in each semester. (Or set an earlier deadline so you can have more focused time for writing papers.) Then you'll have a "base" number of pages to read each day.[3] This ensures you will remain ahead of schedule and adequately prepared for each assignment. Trust me, your studies will be too challenging for you to fall behind.

2. **Chart your course on the front end.** It's fine to avail yourself of student advisors and guidance counselors, but take ownership of your course of study. Wise counsel is helpful, but only you know your strengths, interests, abilities, time commitments, and sense of calling. So take ownership of your academic progress. After all, you are the responsible party.

3. **Sequence your classes wisely.** After determining which classes you'll take, be strategic about when

you take them. Some sequencing is obvious; taking Theology I or Church History I before Theology II or Church History II, for example. Other choices are more subtle. For instance, I would encourage you to take your biblical-survey classes early in your studies. Obtaining a big-picture, working knowledge of the whole Bible will enable you to get the most from other classes. Start broadly, in other words, and narrow your focus as you progress.

4. **Prioritize the biblical languages.** Some topics are easier self-taught than others. For example, you will likely continue growing after seminary by reading books on theology, church history, preaching, and leadership. Hebrew and Greek, however, are far more difficult to learn and maintain on your own. So go as deep with them in seminary as your time, gifting, and degree program permits. And start the languages as early as possible in your degree program. As you do, you'll be able to grow in them throughout your studies.

5. **Know how you learn best.** The famous organizational theorist Peter Drucker wrote extensively on this topic. I've been helped by reading his books; you would be wise to read them, too. Questions to reflect on include: Do you study best at night or in the morning? Are you more of a visual or auditory learner? Do you best retain knowledge by listening, writing notes, or typing? How do you process and review data? Figure out the answers to these questions at the start of your studies to maximize your seminary experience.

6. **Learn to gut a book.** During your first semester, you will likely be stricken by syllabus shock. Assignments to complete, and especially pages to read, will look daunting. You'll quickly discover that you need to be able to

gut a book. This means reading it quickly while still being able to discern the key arguments, follow the supporting evidence, and track the narrative. You also need to develop your own system for note-taking and marking key points on a page.

7. **Home in on your giftings and interests.** Intentionally or not, you will come to realize areas of potential specialization. Some will choose elective courses accordingly, while others will contemplate an additional degree in a preferred field. The most obvious area of delineation is the biblical languages. Some more naturally take to Hebrew; others are better at Greek. For others, neither comes naturally; for even fewer, both do. Your ability to flourish in certain courses may reveal opportunities to advance in those areas.

8. **Attach yourself to key professors.** In higher education, the faculty is the curriculum. Formally, they determine the curriculum by approving degree programs and classes. Practically, they deliver the curriculum by teaching. You will benefit from the faculty's work in the classroom, but also by interacting with them in more personal settings. Most faculty members will be accessible, happy to answer follow-up questions, and willing to offer academic or ministerial encouragement. Make the most of your time with them while you have the opportunity.

> **In higher education, the faculty is the curriculum.**

9. **Devotionalize your studies.** I realize final exams and academic deadlines can complicate this point, but resolve to view all of your classes as a spiritual exercise.

Certain classes, such as exegesis and spiritual formation, will clearly be so. For other classes, the connection won't be as obvious. Regardless, look for concrete ways to apply your learning to your ministry—and to your life.

As I type this chapter, I'm reminded of a conversation I had on campus just last week. I was visiting with about a dozen first-year Master of Divinity students. They are all sharp; most were undergraduate ministry majors. I asked what struck them most about their seminary experience thus far. They all said how much more demanding their seminary studies are over their college experience. This will almost certainly be true of you as well.

Reminding yourself of why you're studying—to know God and to get prepared to faithfully serve Him—will be essential throughout the seminary grind. But while theological education can be daunting, it is also exhilarating and rewarding. What a weighty calling you've received; now go and prepare like it.

Regardless of your past academic achievement, or lack thereof, resolve to immerse yourself in your scholastic pursuits while in seminary. It will be rigorous—and worth it. As Charles Spurgeon famously observed, "Give yourself unto reading. The man who never reads will never be read; he who never quotes will never be quoted. He who will not use the thoughts of other men's brains, proves that he has no brains of his own. You need to read."[4]

# CHAPTER 10

# Know Yourself

John Calvin opened his magnum opus, *The Institutes of the Christian Religion*, with the following words:

> Nearly all the wisdom which we possess, that is to say, true and sound wisdom, consists of two parts: the knowledge of God and of ourselves. But, while joined by many bonds, which one precedes and brings forth the other is not easy to discern.[1]

While the knowledge of God will be a primary topic during your time at seminary, I want to focus now on Calvin's second aspect of true and sound wisdom—the knowledge of oneself. Self-knowledge is a difficult subject to master, isn't it? We see ourselves differently than others do. We gaze outward; others gaze at us. We minister; others observe our ministry. We serve; others assess our service.

Moreover, there's the complication of the *real* self versus the *perceived* self. If we're not careful, we can construct mental realities that are far from accurate. Perhaps we see our gifts in one way, but others see us altogether differently. We're inclined to give ourselves the benefit of the doubt, while others see our actions and afford us no such grace.

All of this reminds us why we should strive to know ourselves better than we do. For this enables a healthier, more fruitful ministry.

## KNOW YOURSELF THEOLOGICALLY

Earlier I referred to my first pastorate, and how it proved to be a joyful experience. But it was *barely* my first pastorate; I dodged a bullet with another church a few months prior, and a little self-awareness was how. Let me explain.

We moved to seminary in late summer 2001. By early 2002 my wife, Karen, was expecting our first child. We had committed to her staying home when the baby arrived. Overlaying that time horizon was a quest for my first pastorate. Our hopes and prayers were that the church would pay us enough so Karen could give her full-time energies to our growing family, and for me to serve the church and continue my studies.

I was reluctant to circulate a résumé, so my approach was a little nontraditional. I met with a few seminary professors, associational directors, state-convention employees, and key pastors to seek their help in finding a church.

A few months into the process, we found ourselves in serious conversation with a church in southern Indiana. It seemed too good to be true. The church was less than an hour from campus, and the ministry expectations were minimal—lead Wednesday night Bible study, preach on Sunday morning, and visit members on Sunday afternoons.

They even said we didn't need to live in the community; remaining in Louisville near the seminary campus was fine. They were also content for me to remain a full-time student and keep my part-time seminary job. Then, they sheepishly said they could only pay me $40,000 per year. Only! That seemed like an unfathomable amount of money—especially for a part-time pastorate. The situation seemed perfect.

I showed up to the final interview with a couple of questions and, in the course of the conversation, it became clear they had female elders. Given my complementarian convictions, this brought added complication to the conversation. I believe the Bible reserves the office of elder for qualified men, so I knew this would be a point of conflict.

I knew serving in that setting would weigh on my conscience. I would either have to serve with a pricked conscience or seek to change their polity—which would likely result in immediate conflict. That self-knowledge prevented me from accepting the pastorate, thereby sparing me (and them) from the inevitable collision that would have soon come.

Now, you may not share my conviction about Scripture's teaching regarding women in pastoral leadership. But, as you contemplate your first ministry position, you need a clear sense of what you believe, why you believe it, and in what ministry settings you are willing to serve. It is unfair to you—and to the place you would minister—to enter a context that compromises your conscience. Know yourself well enough theologically to prevent that from happening.

Seminary is the right setting to crystallize such matters. As you journey through your course of study, you will come into your own theologically. And that's a good thing.

## KNOW YOUR GIFTS

Delivering sermons in a preaching lab can be a humiliating endeavor. Whether it's the artificiality of the environment, the intimidation from the professor, or the critical feedback from "that guy" in class, it's an experience we would prefer to forget.

But the experience is essential, especially for students who haven't had many other opportunities to preach.

Homiletics classes teach you not only how to preach, but, in general, how to deliver God's Word. Such courses should clarify—or at least begin to clarify—your gifting to preach or teach. As we've seen, every pastor must possess at least a baseline ability to study and deliver God's Word. Beyond that baseline gifting, there is a range of ability that varies with each person. Due to a host of factors including gifting, experience, self-discipline, and natural/physical gifts (or lack thereof), ministers are more-or-less proficient in proclamation.

Some enjoy preparing messages and long to preach as much as possible. Others find the study more of a grind, and preaching a daunting responsibility. Seminary is the time to sort out where you fit on the spectrum.

Throughout seminary you should also clarify, as best you can, your aptitude more broadly. Perhaps the Lord has given you a gentle and compassionate spirit that will lend well to counseling in God's church. Or maybe He has given you a desire to disciple and train up the next generation. If so, your first foray into ministry may be focused on student ministry. Perhaps you are detail-oriented and don't necessarily desire a full-time preaching role. You might be suited to be an executive pastor, who largely handles church administration.

My point is not to narrow what the Lord might be leading you to do. I simply want you to discern, in conversation with others, how He has gifted you and how that might be expressed in ministry.

### KNOW YOUR LIMITATIONS

On the flipside, you should also discern your limitations. Again, some are more suited for one ministerial role over another. For me, during seminary and in my earliest season of ministry, I sensed two particular weaknesses—youth ministry and counseling ministry. I love children, including teenagers, but I sensed God had wired me to best minister to adults. I trusted that as I faithfully ministered to parents, it would lead to healthier families and therefore healthier adolescents.

Even by way of personality, I connected better with senior adults than teenagers. I felt more comfortable visiting shut-ins and making hospital visits than hosting lock-ins and pizza parties.

Similarly, I struggled with counseling sessions. To be clear, I believe a pastor must be able to counsel church members. I've maintained that discipline and am genuinely glad to counsel a church member for a session or two. And yet I have often found ongoing sessions to yield diminishing returns for the one I'm trying to help.

For me, then, studying and preparing sermons, leading the congregation and ministry staff, and shepherding families was more natural and aligned with my gifting. In the same way, friend, seize ministry opportunities that will align with your gifts—and dodge those that will depend on your limitations.

## KNOW YOUR TEMPTATIONS

Ministers are not immune to fallenness, and the quicker you detect your own sin patterns and the circumstances in which they tend to arrive, the better. What sins do you struggle with ongoingly? Do lust, pride, envy, bitterness, slothfulness, or gluttony reoccur in your life?

As you grow more aware of these sin patterns, you'll be better equipped to insulate your life from them. Hear me carefully: You will likely struggle with these temptations for the rest of your life. Identifying them does not ensure liberation, but it does enable growth in sanctification. Know your temptations.

## KNOW YOUR AMBITIONS

Ambition is tricky. It is loaded with downsides but, when rightly channeled, can be a source of much kingdom good. What drives you? What animates you? Is it to be well known? To have a large online following? To publish a book? To pastor a megachurch? Such ambitions may prove spiritually hazardous to your ministry and your soul.

The solution, however, is not to be unambitious, but to channel your ambition in God-honoring ways. Set your eyes on knowing His Word, cultivating a deep prayer life, and winning people to Christ. Set your eyes on spiritually minded, kingdom-enhancing targets—and incentivize *those* outcomes.

> **Don't run from your ambition. Redeem it.**

Don't run from your ambition. Redeem it. But keep a vigilant eye on your motives all the while. If you're not careful, you will wake up one day only to realize you've been building your own kingdom instead of Christ's.

## KNOW HOW TO BE YOURSELF

Know who you are, and how to be who you are. God made you, called you, and gifted you to bring Him glory in unique ways. Don't compromise that by trying to be someone else or to replicate another's ministry.

For example, avoid mimicking your favorite preacher. If that's John Piper or Matt Chandler, you'll just sound like a worse version of Piper or Chandler. Listen to many preachers, learn from many podcasts, but be yourself. Cultivate contentment with how God formed and gifted *you*. Rest in that knowledge.

## KNOW WHERE YOU FLOURISH

This one is the trickiest. The point isn't that you should only serve in contexts where you're assured you'll flourish. The point is you should know your gifting, training, and calling enough to sense the kinds of places and roles you're well suited for. Now, God may call you to a place where you will not flourish in order to train you for a future role in which you will. Either way, know yourself well enough to know when and where you will likely thrive.

Learning about yourself can be the most difficult of all studies, but it is essential to vocational excellence and ministerial faithfulness. Your spouse can be exceedingly helpful here. He or she likely knows you better than anyone and will be comfortable speaking directly with you. Invite your spouse into these conversations. Reflect together on your strengths and weaknesses, in what context you flourish, and how the Lord has gifted you.

The conversation might be awkward at first, but your spouse will feel honored that you initiated it. And long after the awkwardness fades, you will be the beneficiary because you will better know yourself.

# CHAPTER 11

# Develop a Band of Brothers (or Sisters)

The opportunity to build ministry friendships was one of the most unexpected but pleasant surprises of my MDiv studies. I knew pastors who spoke glowingly of friendships forged in seminary, but I had not yet experienced a depth of ministry relationships.

Seminary, I soon found, is particularly conducive to such friendships. The crucible of studies, the shared hardships, the uniqueness of the call, the trials and triumphs—all these tend to make seminary friendships long-lasting ones.

When Karen and I moved to Louisville and settled into our off-campus apartment, we noticed a young man, apparently from India, who lived beneath us. We would pass him on the stairwell or bump into him in the parking lot. He was always warm and engaging. In the evenings when he cooked, the aroma of curry would waft upstairs. I assumed he had immigrated to America for academic or employment opportunities.

Karen and I desired to share the gospel with him, so after a few weeks getting settled into our apartment, we invited him up for dinner. What followed makes me smile to this day.

Over dinner I began to unpack the gospel, how Christ had changed our lives, and that we moved to Louisville for ministry preparation. In slightly broken English he said, "I Christian. I a Calvinist. I study at Southern Seminary, too."

In the ensuing months, Anant became a good friend, enriching our lives and opening my eyes to global Christianity. While studying at seminary, you will likely have similar experiences—but it will take some intentionality on your part.

## LIFE TOGETHER

Published in 1939, Dietrich Bonhoeffer's *Life Together* is a classic on Christian community. Seminaries have pointed to it for generations as the gold standard for discipleship in community.

> **Isolation is a breeding ground for sin; community is how we thrive amid the trials and joys of the Christian life.**

The book's beauty is accentuated by Bonhoeffer's own life and ministry. Laboring in the crucible of Nazi Germany, his prophetic ministry would cost him his life. Here's what the German pastor observed:

It is not simply to be taken for granted that the Christian has the privilege of living among other Christians. Jesus Christ lived in the midst of his enemies. At the end, the disciples deserted him. On the cross, he was utterly alone, surrounded by evildoers and mockers. . . . So the Christian, too, belongs not in the seclusion of a cloistered life but in the thick of foes. . . . between the death of Christ and the Last Day it is only by a gracious anticipation of the last things that Christians are privileged to live in visible fellowship with other Christians.[1]

Bonhoeffer poignantly exposes the truth that the Christian life is not meant to be lived alone. Isolation is a breeding ground for sin; community is how we thrive amid the trials and joys of the Christian life. Reflecting on the apostle Paul's relationships, Bonhoeffer writes:

The physical presence of other Christians is a source of incomparable joy and strength to the believer. Lovingly, the imprisoned apostle Paul calls his "dearly beloved son in the faith," Timothy, to come to him in prison in the last days of his life; he would see him again and have him near. Paul has not forgotten the tears Timothy shed when last they parted (II Tim 1:4). Remembering the congregation in Thessalonica, Paul prays "night and day . . . exceedingly that we may see your face" (I Thess. 3:10). The aged John knows that this joy will not be full until he can come to his own people and speak face to face instead of writing with ink (II John 12).[2]

Christian community and true spiritual brotherhood is an unusual gift, but it shouldn't be. And yet it takes work. Here are some practical ways to cultivate such friendships:

1. **Know your professors.** Your professors will not only be a source of encouragement in seminary but also a resource throughout your ministry. I often hear graduates reflect warmly on reaching out to a former professor about an exegetical question or church issue and, though it's been years since they graduated, the professor was eager to help. Additionally, professors are

well positioned to connect you with other like-minded students.

2. **Attend community activities.** I occasionally interact with a student who feels isolated in their studies. When I inquire as to their level of community involvement, it typically becomes clear they aren't invested at all. Hiding out in the back of the library may be good for your grades, but it's not the way to forge friendships. So find a balance. Prioritize both. All work and no play will make you a dull, and lonely, student.

3. **Be a friend.** As we tell our children, to have a friend you must be a friend. Share your notes with a classmate or initiate a study group. More personally, invite a new student to lunch or coordinate an outing as families. Oftentimes, it takes putting oneself out there to develop real friendships. You'll be surprised how quickly a few nice gestures will be rewarded.

4. **Intentionally make friends.** For some of you, making friends will not be a problem at all. You are naturally extroverted and strike up conversations anywhere you go. For others of you, it may be more challenging to make friends. Your tendency may be to develop one or two really good friends but remain closed off to most everyone else. Regardless of how you're wired, be intentional in your friendships.

5. **Utilize technology.** I have a love/hate relationship with social media, but one way it has proven helpful is expanding my circle of friends. In fact, I sometimes have difficulty differentiating between actual relationships and virtual ones. Social media will allow you to connect with seminary peers, which can be particularly helpful if you are an online student. Zoom, FaceTime, and video sessions are more personal, of course, and thus

more conducive to relationship-building than email or an occasional phone call. As in all things, know yourself and use wisdom here. Nothing can substitute for flesh-and-blood relationships, especially in your local church.

6. **Loiter before and after events.** The most important time in seminary may well be the ten minutes before and after chapel. In that gathering, you will have access to most all of the seminary faculty, staff, and administration. It is also a natural gathering place for other students and a natural place to connect. If able, show up early and visit with other students. Ask

> **Nothing can substitute for flesh-and-blood relationships, especially in your local church.**

where they came from and what they are studying. Additionally, stay after and discuss the sermon or your current classes. This little bit of small talk can be the first step in developing more meaningful relationships.

7. **Be intentional about similarity.** Commonalities are a natural point of connection and, therefore, of community. You will likely connect more quickly with other students from your home church, home state, or undergraduate college. Moreover, similar life stage is also a natural connection point. If you're married with young children, you will probably gravitate toward other students with the same. Lastly, those who are like-minded academically in study habits or theological affinities will have more natural connections. This is not a bad thing; just be mindful of what draws you together.

8. **Be intentional about dissimilarity.** A failure to be intentional here will limit your relational and

community network. Cultivate relationships with students of different ethnicities, from different regions, with different theological interests and ministry pursuits. By this simple step, you will be amazed at how much your perspective is informed and broadened. And as you get to know people who are dissimilar, you'll be encouraged by the size and diversity of God's kingdom.

The phrase "band of brothers" gained cultural traction in the early 2000s when Steven Spielberg and Tom Hanks teamed up to create the World War II miniseries of the same name. Before then, military leaders like Admiral Horatio Nelson had used the term to refer to colleagues in arms. The phrase actually originated with William Shakespeare who, in his St. Crispin's Day Speech of *Henry V*, wrote,

We few, we happy few, we band of brothers;
For he today that sheds his blood with me
Shall be my brother; be he ne'er so vile,
This day shall gentle his condition.[3]

For twenty-first-century ministers in the West, bloodshed in arms is an almost unheard-of experience. Yet something even more grueling faces us. Spiritual warfare is constant, the evil one relentless in attack. The peaks and valleys of ministry are a never-ending slog.

Ministers who endure to the end do so with the help of a band of brothers or sisters—close friends from whom they find encouragement, accountability, and strength. You need this not only for the ministry that comes after your studies but for the ministry that is your studies. Seminary can be the incubator for such friendships. Make sure it is for you.

# Get Placed

I grew up in a sports-oriented family. My father played high-school basketball and had the opportunity to play in college. My mother appreciated sports and was happy to shuttle us to practices and root for us from the stands. I suppose my older brothers and I were predestined to be athletes.

From childhood, little-league baseball and church-league basketball were a part of our lives. Given our height, abilities, and desires, we focused on basketball during our teenage years. My two brothers (six and eight years older) both became high-school basketball stars and went on to play in college. One of them, Marc, even earned NAIA All-American honors and enjoyed a stint of professional basketball in Europe.

As my brothers distinguished themselves in high school, I rooted for them and envisioned a basketball trajectory similar to theirs. They were tall; so was I. They loved the game; so did I. Their last name was Allen; so was mine. They were successful; I would be, too—or so I thought.

As clear as day, I recall a clarifying conversation with my father as I approached my teens. He said, in effect, you don't just walk on the court one day and announce yourself a college athlete. College basketball is a finishing point, not a starting point. The process starts now—in the backyard, in the weight room, in the gym. It takes years of preparation and toil to become a college basketball player.

The conversation landed on me like a ton of bricks. It was sobering. It was, in the near-term, discouraging, but it also proved motivating. As I digested it, it launched me on a trajectory of focus and self-discipline that led to multiple basketball-scholarship offers.

Before that conversation, I was merely a hypothetical college athlete. After that conversation, I was on a trajectory to become one. Ministry is like this, too.

### HYPOTHETICAL MINISTERS NEED NOT APPLY

Over the years, I have noticed a certain type of student I'd call a hypothetical minister. Their studies for ministry, in effect, become their ministry. Church attendance becomes sporadic; church service nonexistent.

In fact, this type of student often develops a critical spirit toward the church. They spot its weaknesses a mile away, are keen on critiquing it, and even more on lecturing others about how it should operate. If you think like this, you should heed Spurgeon's correction:

> The church is not perfect, but woe to the man who finds pleasure in pointing out her imperfections! Christ loved his church, and let us do the same. I have no doubt that the Lord can see more fault in his church than I can; and I have equal confidence that he sees no fault at all. Because he covers her faults with his own love—that love which covers a multitude of sins; and he removes all her defilement with that precious blood which washes away all the transgressions of his people.[1]

We all know of unhealthy churches worthy of criticism, but that shouldn't breed a class of professional church critics. Left unchecked, such cynicism can grow corrosive, hardening one's heart toward the church and sapping one's desire to serve it.

This type of person becomes a hypothetical minister. In the abstract, they're willing to serve the church; but they rarely do. They have trouble finding a church that meets their standards or is worthy of their service.

For a seminary student, this is a deeply unhealthy state to be in—but it also has long-

**If asked about your service to the local church during seminary, to struggle coming up with an answer is not a good place to be.**

term liabilities. Most churches are not looking for a minister with a credential; they are looking for a minister with experience. Having both is best, but experience often beats out formal training. If asked about your service to the local church during seminary, to struggle coming up with an answer is not a good place to be.

Whether due to a critical spirit, indifference, or just a lack of intentionality, you will be disadvantaged if you make it through seminary without gaining ministry experience. It will shortchange your preparation and, most likely, hinder your ability to get placed in a ministry position after seminary. Consider these steps, then, to help you get placed in ministry during seminary:

1. **Find a ministry.** Not every church can afford another staff member, but every church needs another servant. Every prisoner needs a chaplain; every shut-in needs a visitor; every Sunday school class needs a teacher;

everyone hurt needs someone to pray. Be strategic about meeting ministry needs—and be sure to capture that experience on paper. Now, you shouldn't cultivate ulterior motives. The last thing I want is for you to serve just to pad your résumé. Rather, I want you to be deliberate about serving because you love Christ and His church. But as God opens doors, record what you've done for future use. Even a little experience is better than none at all.

**Not every church can afford another staff member, but every church needs another servant.**

**2. Be strategic about your church membership.** Typically the best place to get ministry experience will be the church you're a member of. If you're changing churches due to a move to seminary, or for some other reason, discuss with the pastor your desire for experience and how he can envision you gaining it. If you're looking for a church in your seminary town, keep this in mind as well. Will this potential church have real opportunities for you to serve, or will you be one of thirty seminary students vying to teach a Sunday school class? While it's certainly not wrong to be in a church with many capable leaders, it may be worth driving an extra twenty minutes to serve one that desperately needs the help.

**3. Seek out advocates.** Whether it be a pastor, a professor, a regional ministry leader, or a church-placement officer, find others who will help you get placed. Most pastors have been where you are now. They know your struggles and apprehensions. They find joy in helping freshly minted ministers—but they cannot help you if they do not know you. Seek out advocates and avail yourself of their help and advice. In ministry, much like the rest of the world, it matters who you know. Again, I'm not advocating for extreme networking or self-promotion; I'm just saying there's nothing wrong with sending your CV to associational leaders and asking to get a cup of coffee to discuss potential churches with openings. There's a big difference between the two approaches.

**4. Maintain truth in advertising.** In 2001, Notre Dame —one of America's most storied college-football programs—hired a new head coach. But his tenure lasted only five days. The new coach resigned when a reporter discovered that he had padded his résumé. Whatever you do, don't do that. Be honest about the experience you have—and don't have. Additionally, be honest about your theological convictions, your spiritual autobiography, and your leadership style. A pure heart and a tender conscience will always win the day. Remember that ministry is ultimately about serving the Lord, who sees all. Do you think the Lord will bless you or your ministry if you had to lie or fudge the truth to get it?

**5. Get fired in the interview.** No matter how desperate you are for a position, don't pursue it under false pretenses. Résumé juicing is one form of false pretense; another is not speaking candidly about your convictions, experience, and leadership intentions. You have a moral responsibility to the church to be clear about these things. If it's a deal-breaker, it's a deal-breaker. Believe me, it is a thousand times better to get fired in the interview than shortly after taking the position. The former might give you a bad day; the latter, a bad year— if not more. Lord willing, there will be another church that has more like-minded convictions. Be patient as you wait.

6. **Be flexible, but know yourself.** As we've discussed, self-awareness is important in life and ministry. Early opportunities may be outside your comfort zone and not align with what you hope to be your long-term ministry trajectory. That's fine. During your early season of ministry, you'll better discern what God has called you to do—and not do. That said, don't take on a ministry task that's fundamentally outside of your gifting and interests. If you're not energized by other people's children, don't become a children's minister. If you're not gifted to preach, then a position where you're responsible for three sermons a week is a sure way to kill your ministry. As I've conveyed throughout this book, it all comes down to wisdom, discernment, and knowing yourself. There is nothing wrong with taking a less-than-ideal position early on in ministry, but if you know the position won't be fruitful for you or for the church, then it's better just to wait.

7. **Reach for the doorknob, but let God open the door.** Every person has to operate in accordance with his or her own conscience. One's level of comfort with networking, résumé circulation, and requesting strategic recommendations will vary. But even if you're comfortable reaching for the doorknob, let the Lord open the door. If He has called you, He has a plan for you. You don't have to sit idle, but you shouldn't play God either.

Looking back, I sort of fell into my first real ministry experience. Dr. Steve Lawson—then pastor of Dauphin Way Baptist Church in Mobile, Alabama—invited me to serve as an intern, which later developed into a full-time position. I had no experience or credentials. In fact, nothing obviously commended me to the position.

But I was eager. I arrived early to church services and lingered late. I sat toward the front, took copious notes, and often reviewed those notes with Dr. Lawson. I tried not to be a nuisance, but I did ask questions about preaching, sermon preparation, theology, and ministry. I had neither formal training nor experience; all I had was eagerness. Yet eagerness is better than nothing at all.

Churches often look for experience more than they look for a credential. That's what they desire, and that is what you need. The best way to get a ministry position, then, is to have one. It is always easier to go somewhere in ministry from somewhere in ministry. So be intentional and be placed.

# Seminary Is a Step of Faith. Take It!

A s a boy growing up on the Alabama Gulf Coast, we literally lived on the water, our homes situated on coastal lots. Fishing, skiing, and boating were daily parts of life. To this day, few things bring me more pleasure than being back on the water. It isn't just rejuvenating; it's nostalgic. It brings back a flood of sweet memories, times I now enjoy reliving and re-creating with my own children.

Picture with me a dock with a boat floating six feet away. Before you attempt to board, you pull the boat as close to you as possible, so as to safely step in. You don't think much about crossing the few-inch gap. If young and agile, you may even be comfortable hopping several feet. Unless it's an emergency, though, you would never try hopping several yards. You would likely wind up wet, if not injured.

But there comes a time when, if you're going to go boating, you have to actually step over into the boat. Yes, it's prudent to pull the boat close and cross the gap with balance and care. But you have to take the step.

**You should pray, plan, prepare, and take every other prudential step—but it remains a step of faith.**

So it is with seminary. You should pray, plan, prepare, and take every other prudential step —but it remains a step of faith. Don't let fear or uncertainty delay you. Rather, trust the Lord's objective and subjective indicators that ministry, and ministry preparation, should be in your future. Then take the step of faith.

## TRUST YOUR CALLING

If you believe and see these internal and external confirmations that God has called you to ministry, then seminary training is the next logical step. (If you remain unsettled in your calling, let me point you to my book *Discerning Your Call to Ministry*,[1] which will help you gain clarity.)

If you are certain, rest in that calling. Know that God has set you apart to serve His church and to advance His gospel. He has a special ministerial plan for your life. The journey will be hard, but it will be spiritually rich and eternally consequential. You can trust your calling, friend, because you know and trust the One who issued it.

## TRUST YOUR CHURCH

As we have discussed, no call to ministry is an individual undertaking. The Holy Spirit implants the desire, but the local church assesses and affirms the calling. As Brian Croft puts it, "It is the local church that God has appointed to be the agent to test, train, affirm and send those who are called."[2] If your church knows you, has observed you, and has affirmed your character and gifting, you should gain confidence in your calling by remembering *their* confidence in your calling.

Your pastor or elders will be doubly important in this process. As you gather their support for your ministry pursuit and their affirmation for your seminary studies, it should profoundly reassure you. Trust your church, and especially those who lead it.

## TRUST YOUR SPOUSE

If you're married, the most important person in your life is your spouse. You cannot undertake ministry—or seminary training—without their support, and you should not try. Yes, it may take time, prayer, conversation, and deliberation for them to warm to the idea. This will especially be the case if God calls you midlife and your spouse is accustomed to different living circumstances.

Seminary will not just cost you money and time; it will also cost your *spouse* money and time. Spiritually, then, you must have spousal support. Practically, I couldn't imagine undertaking seminary without it. Conversely, as you have his or her support, and as he or she believes in your calling and is willing to sacrifice for your ministry preparation, it should embolden you. Trust your spouse.

## TRUST GOD'S WORD

From cover to cover, your Bible is true and trustworthy. It is pregnant with promises, many of which pertain to submitting to God's will, following His call, surrendering to His plan, and pursuing His directives. Along with those promises, it should be added, come warnings for those who resist His leadership.

I encourage you to trace God's scriptural promises related

> **Do not enter seminary doubting God. Gain conviction and confidence in Him from Holy Scripture. His Word is good, and you can trust it.**

to ministry service, His care for prophets and preachers, and His assurances of blessing for those who sacrifice for Him. Do not enter seminary doubting God. Gain conviction and confidence in Him from Holy Scripture. His Word is good, and you can trust it.

## TRUST YOUR SEMINARY

One sign you're considering the right institution is that you can trust it. (If you cannot, find one you can.) You should be able to trust it at every level, especially theologically. You should also be able to trust its admissions officers, guidance counselors, financial-aid advisors, and other seminary personnel.

Of course, seminary personnel believe in their institution and are persuasive in promoting it. Admissions officers aren't paid to talk people *out* of coming, after all. But upright institutions do not coerce. At Midwestern Seminary, we often deny or delay admission to students for spiritual, academic, or other wise reasons. Though not the ultimate arbiters, your pursuit of seminary can be reinforced by an institution that finds you worthy of admission. Find a seminary you can trust.

## TRUST THE LORD!

Finally, and most importantly, trust the Lord who called you. He promised to build His church, and He's done so for two thousand years. He promised to raise up ministers and missionaries for His church, and He's done so for two thousand years. The Lord's church is unstoppable. His commitment to calling out ministers is undeterred.

If He is calling you, therefore, know you have the authority of Christ behind you, the power of Christ within you, and the message of Christ upon you. The risen Lord has never failed His church or His ministers—and He is not going to start with you.

Let me end this book by dispelling a common notion that hinders many from attending seminary *now*. It is so easy to think the *next* season of life will prove simpler, less complicated, or more conducive to seminary training.

> **The Lord's church is unstoppable. His commitment to calling out ministers is undeterred.**

For most all of us, however, that is just not the case.

Life's responsibilities and opportunities tend to grow with each passing year, not shrink. In the years ahead, you will likely have more relationships to maintain, more individuals to care for, more financial needs to meet, more family obligations to manage, and more life responsibilities to juggle.

Children are glorious additions, but they require significant time and financial support. As they age, those two factors only increase. There's just never a "perfect" time to start. If God is calling you, and you are not providentially impaired, take the plunge and start seminary.

---

At the end of your life, you'll not likely wish things had been easier, or that you'd attained more money, notoriety, or material items. If you have regrets, they'll likely involve wishing you were more eternally minded. Refocus now. Keep your eyes on Christ. Remember this is not your home; you have been called to a higher purpose.

Part of succeeding at seminary is securing these truths at the front of your mind. If you can keep this big picture in view, your motivation will not wane, and your time in seminary will bear fruit. To this end, I'll leave you with one of my favorite quotes, often attributed to C. T. Studd:

> Only one life, 'twill soon be past,
> Only what's done for Christ will last.

# Acknowledgments

L ike every book project, this one could not have come to completion without many who've given much.

At the personal level, my life and ministry is enriched beyond measure by my family. God has abundantly blessed me with a wife in Karen, and children in Anne-Marie, Caroline, William, Alden, and Elizabeth, who have surpassed my every hope and dream as to who they'd become and mean to me. They are a constant source of love, joy, and support.

In fact, my children have lived the story and message of this book with me. During the course of my seminary studies, Karen birthed our five children. When God called us to Midwestern Seminary, they were ages 4–9. Now, as I tidy up this book project, they're ages 12–18. Their lives have been lived, one way or another, in a seminary context. In large part with them, through them, and because of them, the story and message of this book exists.

Thus, to my favorite six people on the planet, thank you.

At the institutional level, my colleagues and office staff likewise are an invaluable source of support and encouragement. Most especially, I'm thankful for Tyler Sykora, Dawn Philbrick, and Lauren Hansen. Additionally, I'm thankful for Wesley Rule, who assisted in the project. These men and women are an absolute delight to serve with, and they go about their daily tasks with graciousness and professionalism. Thank you.

Furthermore, I'm thankful to the team at Moody Publishers, most especially Drew Dyck and Connor Sterchi, who are great to partner with.

Last, and most of all, I'm indebted to my Lord and Savior, Jesus Christ. Like every other ministerial undertaking, none of this would be possible without His grace, calling, and enabling. May this book, and all that I do, bring Him much glory—and His church better prepared, more faithful servants.

# Notes

### Chapter 1: Celebrate and Clarify Your Call

1. Moody Bible Institute's *Today in the Word*, November 1989, 7.

2. Jason K. Allen, *Discerning Your Call to Ministry: How to Know for Sure and What to Do about It* (Chicago: Moody, 2016).

### Chapter 2: Prepare for Three Years, Get Prepared for Thirty

1. John Piper, *Brothers, We Are Not Professionals: A Plea to Pastors for Radical Ministry* (Nashville: B&H Publishing Group, 2013), 1.

2. Kevin DeYoung, "Why the Church Still Needs the Seminary," The Gospel Coalition, https://www.thegospelcoalition.org/blogs/ kevin-deyoung/why-the-church-still-needs-the-seminary.

### Chapter 3: Pick the Right Institution: What to Look For and Why It Matters

1. John Piper, "Choosing a Seminary," Ask Pastor John, Desiring God, May 13, 2013, https://www.desiringgod.org/interviews/ choosing-a-seminary.

2. For more information on the Cooperative Program, please visit http://www.sbc.net/cp.

3. Each of these issues will be treated in more depth in chapter eight, "Plan Your Finances."

4. Piper, "Choosing a Seminary."

## Chapter 5: Guard Your Life and Your Doctrine

1. D. A. Carson, *Exegetical Fallacies* (Grand Rapids, MI: Baker Academic, 1996), 23.

2. Ibid., 23.

3. B. B. Warfield, *The Religious Life of Theological Students* (Phillipsburg, NJ: P&R, 1983), 2, emphasis added.

4. For more on the spiritual disciplines, see Donald S. Whitney's *Spiritual Disciplines of the Christian Life* (Colorado Springs: NavPress, 2014).

5. David Mathis and Jonathan Parnell, *How to Stay Christian in Seminary* (Wheaton, IL: Crossway, 2014).

## Chapter 6: Steward Your Time—It's Your Most Valuable Asset

1. Peter T. O'Brien, *The Letter to the Ephesians*, *Pillar New Testament Commentary* (Grand Rapids, MI: Eerdmans, 1999), 382, emphasis mine.

2. Ibid., 383.

3. Stephen R. Covey, *The Seven Habits of Highly Effective People: Powerful Lessons in Personal Change* (New York: Free Press, 2004), 136–37.

4. John Maxwell, quoted in Dave Ramsey, *The Money Answer Book* (Nashville: Thomas Nelson, 2010), 87.

## Chapter 7: Get an A at Home, Even if It Means a C in Class

1. Robert W. Yarbrough, *The Letters to Timothy and Titus*, Pillar New Testament Commentary (Grand Rapids, MI: Eerdmans, 2018), 198–99.

2. You can read more about the Midwestern Women's Institute at https://www.mbts.edu/current-students/mwi.

3. Matthew Henry, "A Church in the House" (New York: American Tract Society, 1824), 50, 53.

## Chapter 8: Plan Your Finances

1. Dave Ramsey, *The Total Money Makeover: A Proven Plan for Financial Fitness* (Nashville: Thomas Nelson, 2013).

2. Art Rainer, *The Money Challenge: 30 Days of Discovering God's Design for You and Your Money* (Nashville: B&H, 2017).

3. Larry Burkett, *How to Manage Your Money: An In-Depth Bible Study on Personal Finances* (Chicago: Moody, 2002).

## Chapter 9: Hit the Books

1. Donald Guthrie, *Pastoral Epistles: An Introduction and Commentary*, vol. 14, *Tyndale New Testament Commentaries* (Downers Grove, IL: InterVarsity Press, 1990), 164–65.

2. R. C. Sproul, *Knowing Scripture* (Downers Grove, IL: InterVarsity Press, 2009), 20.

3. For example, if you have 5,000 pages of reading to complete in a 16-week semester, then you would divide 5,000 by 112 (16 weeks is 112 days). But, let's say you want to have your reading completed in 13 weeks so you can have extra time to work on your final papers. Then, you would divide 5,000 by 91, which equals roughly 55. So, according to this plan, you could have all your reading done in 13 weeks by reading 55 pages a day.

4. *The Complete Works of C. H. Spurgeon*, vol. 9, Sermons 487 to 546 (Harrington, DE: Delmarva Publications, 2013).

## Chapter 10: Know Yourself

1. John Calvin, *Institutes of the Christian Religion*, I.1.i.

## Chapter 11: Develop a Band of Brothers (or Sisters)

1. Dietrich Bonhoeffer, *Life Together: The Classic Exploration of Christian Community* (New York: HarperCollins, 1954), 17–18.

2. Ibid., 19.

3. William Shakespeare, *Henry V*, IV. 3. 62–65.

## Chapter 12: Get Placed

1. *The Complete Works of C. H. Spurgeon, Volume 30: Sermons 1757–1815* (Harrington, DE: Delmarva Publications, 2015).

## Conclusion: Seminary Is a Step of Faith. Take It!

1. Jason K. Allen, *Discerning Your Call to Ministry: How to Know for Sure and What to Do about It* (Chicago: Moody, 2016).

2. Brian Croft, quoted in *The Call to Ministry* (Louisville, KY: Southern Baptist Theological Seminary Press, 2013), 14, https://sbts-wordpress-uploads.s3.amazonaws.com/sbts/uploads/2014/05/CO-385-2013-Are-you-called-Journal-Writeable.pdf.

# AS A PASTOR,
## DO YOU FEEL LIKE YOU'RE
## WEARING TOO MANY HATS?

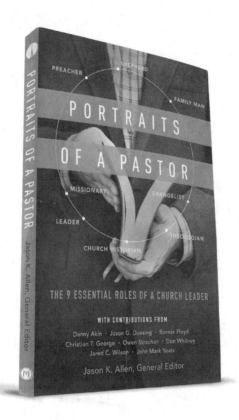

Ministry throws unexpected challenges at you.
What if a little more training could help you
navigate them successfully?

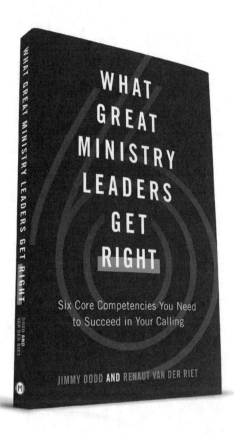

In *What Great Ministry Leaders Get Right*, Jimmy
Dodd and Renaut van der Riet outline the six core
competencies church leaders need to develop healthy,
biblical, and sustainable leadership. Whether you've
been in the pulpit for years or are just beginning your
ministry education, every pastor can make sure they're
prepared for the real-world challenges of ministry.

978-0-8024-2313-9   |   also available as an eBook

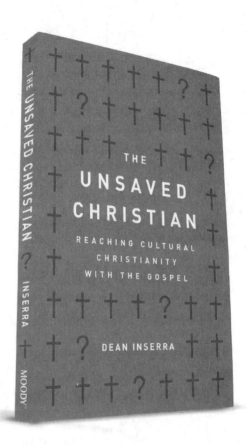